A BANTAM PATHFINDER EDITION

👉 HERE, THEN, 👈
ARE THE FIRST THREE PLAYS
I WROTE FOR MY
PANDEMONIUM THEATRE COMPANY.

Why such a company name? Because it pleased and delighted me. Because it was an unexpected and frivolous name to give a company of glad fools. And because it meant when you came into our theater, you never knew what special kind of hell might break loose.

—Ray Bradbury

BANTAM PATHFINDER EDITIONS

Bantam Pathfinder Editions provide the best in fiction and nonfiction in a wide variety of subject areas. They include novels by classic and contemporary writers; vivid, accurate histories and biographies; authoritative works in the sciences; collections of short stories, plays and poetry.

Bantam Pathfinder Editions are carefully selected and approved. They are durably bound, printed on specially selected high-quality paper, and presented in a new and handsome format.

THE WONDERFUL
ICE CREAM SUIT
AND OTHER PLAYS

BY RAY BRADBURY

BANTAM PATHFINDER EDITIONS
TORONTO / NEW YORK / LONDON

A NATIONAL GENERAL COMPANY

RLI: VLM 4 (VLR 3–4)
        ————————————
        IL 7–up

THE WONDERFUL ICE CREAM SUIT AND OTHER PLAYS
A Bantam Book / published April 1972

Published simultaneously in the United States and Canada

Bantam Books are published by Bantam Books, Inc., a National
General company. Its trade-mark, consisting of the words "Bantam
Books" and the portrayal of a bantam, is registered in the United
States Patent Office and in other countries. Marca Registrada.
Bantam Books, Inc., 666 Fifth Avenue, New York, N.Y. 10019.

PRINTED IN THE UNITED STATES OF AMERICA

CONTENTS

INTRODUCTION
With Notes on Staging

First things first. This book is dedicated to Charles Rome Smith, who has directed all of my work for the theater so far, and who will, God allowing, direct more in the years ahead.

As for myself, I began with the theater and I shall probably end with it. I have not, up to now, made a penny, nickel or dime at it, but my love is constant and, in best cliché fashion, its own reward. It has to be. For no one stands about in the alleys after a show giving doughnut money to crazy playwrights.

My first dream in life was to become a magician. Blackstone summoned me up on stage when I was ten to help him with various illusions. I assisted in vanishing a bird in its cage, and helped stir a rabbit out of a strange omelet. Blackstone gave me the rabbit, which I carried home in happy hysterics. Named Tillie, the rabbit in short order produced six more rabbits and I was off and running as an illusionist.

At twelve I was singing leads in school operettas. At twelve and one-half, in Tucson, Arizona, I announced to my classmates that within two weeks I would be an actor broadcasting from local Radio Station KGAR. Self-propelled by my own infernal brass, I trotted over to the station, hung about emptying ashtrays, running for cokes, and being happily underfoot. Rather than drown me with a batch of kittens, the station gave up and hired me to read the Sunday comics to the kiddies every Saturday night. My pay was free tickets to the local theaters to see *The Mummy* and *King Kong*. I was undoubtedly overpaid.

In high school I wrote the Annual Student Talent Show. At nineteen I belonged to Laraine Day's Wilshire Players Guild in a Mormon Church only a block from my home in Los Angeles. For Laraine, who was becoming a big star at MGM in those days in such films as *My Son, My Son,* I wrote a number of three-act plays that were so incredibly bad no one in the Guild dared tell me of my absolute lack of talent.

Nevertheless, I sensed my own mediocrity and quit playwriting. I vowed never to return to the theater for twenty years, until I had seen and read most of the plays of our time. I lived up to that vow. Only in my late thirties, with thousands of seen performances in my blood, did I dare to try my hand at theater work again.

Even then, licking my old wounds, I feared to let my plays fall into the hands of directors and actors. I seriously doubted my ability, and probably would have delayed additional years had not a friend, hearing of my one-act Irish plays, invited me over to his house one night for a reading. My work was read aloud by actors James Whitmore and Strother Martin. By the end of the evening, we were all on the floor, laughing. Suddenly I realized that the older Bradbury was at long last ready for the theater again.

The theater, however, was not ready for me.

I could find no group, no director, no actor, no banker, prepared to put my plays on a stage.

Only in 1963, when Charles Rome Smith and I fell into each others arms, did I begin to think of producing the plays, myself.

Now this, in itself, is extraordinary. In the entire history of the American theater, only a handful of playwrights have been brash enough, and dumb enough, to save their money and invest it in their own plays.

I talked it over with my wife, told her I thought the plays were more than good, that all the producers were wrong, as well as the bankers, and that I had to try, just once, to see whether or not I was the grandest fool of all.

We saved our money for a year, rented the Coronet Theatre in Los Angeles, finished three one-act plays, hired Charles Rome Smith to direct, and began casting.

The evening of one acts titled *The World of Ray Bradbury*, opened in October, 1964. The reviews were all, I repeat all, excellent. If I had written them myself they couldn't have been better.

The World ran twenty weeks, after which we opened *The Wonderful Ice Cream Suit* for a run of twenty-four weeks, again to incredibly fine notices.

We took *The World of Ray Bradbury* to New York in 1965 where, with inferior casting and a dreary theater in a bad section of the Bowery, plus a newspaper strike which insured our nonexistence, we folded within three nights, to the tune of $40,000 and thirty-five belated and truly bad reviews, published after our closing, when the newspapers rushed back on the scene to give us a dark burial.

I took the slow train home, vowing to stay away from New York for another lifetime. So far, producers and directors in New York appear to feel the same way; I have not been invited East since.

What did I learn from these experiences?

That working with your own group, your own theater, your own director, your own actors, your own money, is best.

Working with an outside producer and outside money, one is constantly victimized by worries over losing their investment or toadying to their taste and will.

Working as your own producer, all the fun that *should* be in the theater comes to the surface. I have rarely had such a glorious time in my life. I dearly loved being with my actors and my director. I enjoyed the challenge of casting. I wrote most of the publicity for the theater myself, helped design the advertising, clean out the restrooms, and, finally, take the losses without a sigh or remorseful tear. Strange to report, losing one's own money doesn't hurt at all. Losing other people's money is, for me, anyway, a dreadful experience, one I hope to suffer rarely in a lifetime.

What else did I learn? To trust my own intuitive judgment and taste. Let me give you an example:

My director called me in the midst of rehearsals of *To the Chicago Abyss*. The actors, he cried, are in rebellion. The play won't work they say. Chaos. Tell everyone to hold still, sit down, I'll be right there, I said. I grabbed a taxi and made it to the theater in ten minutes. Okay, I said, everyone on stage, run through the play!

The actors, grumbling, did the play.

When it was over I gave one hell of a yell.

Good grief, you're terrific! I said. You know what's wrong with you? You're all exhausted. You've been in rehearsal four weeks and you don't know which end is up. Let me tell you: this play is the best play of the three we're putting on. It's the play that will get the best notices. In this play, *you* will get the critical shouts of joy.

I was right of course, and my actors were wrong.

The day after our opening, the reviews mentioned *To the Chicago Abyss* above all the other plays. Harold Gould, our principal actor, got raves for his performance as the Old Man Who Remembered Mediocrities.

I guess what I'm saying here is, if you don't have taste, if you don't trust your intuition, if you don't believe in your plays and their ideas to start with, you shouldn't be in the theater. But if you do make the move, make it on your own, save up your money, it doesn't have to be a large amount, rent a warehouse, nail together a ramshackle stage, and do the damned play! I have spent as little as $49.50 producing one of my plays at a storefront theater in Los Angeles. At other times I have spent $200 and then again $20,000, which went into our final production of *The World of R.B.*

For what other reasons did I come back to the theater after almost twenty years away?

Because most of the plays I saw or read in those twenty years had no ideas in them.

Because most of the plays I saw or read had no language, no poetry in them.

I could not then, I cannot now, accept a theater that is devoid of ideas and poetry.

It seemed shocking to me that a country that has been built on ideas, both political and technological, a country that has influenced the entire world with its concepts and three-dimensional extrusions of those concepts in robot forms, would be so singularly lacking in the theater of ideas.

I have always thought that Bernard Shaw deserved to be the patron saint of the American theater. Yet I saw little of his influence here, a true playwright of ideas born to set the world right. Avant-garde in 1900, he remains light years ahead of our entire avant-garde today.

My other saint would be Shakespeare, of course; and I saw none of his best influence at work in our theater arts.

They say that novelists write the books they wish they could find in libraries.

I set out to write the plays I did not see on the American stage. Shaw? No. Shakespeare? Hardly. Yet if one's influences are not great and broad and wondrous, one has nowhere to start and nowhere to go. These fine ghosts were my instructors, my good company, my friends.

I rediscovered them through Charles Laughton.

In 1955, Charles Laughton and Paul Gregory asked me to adapt my novel *Fahrenheit 451* to the stage. I came up with a bad play. Laughton and Gregory gave me drinks one night at sunset and told me just how bad, but told me kindly. A few months later, Charlie had me up to his house. He stood on his hearth and began to talk about theater, about Molière, about the Restoration playwrights, but particularly about Shaw and then Shakespeare.

As he talked, his house filled with pageantry. The flagstones of his fireplace knew the print of horses and the cry of mobs. The theater of Shakespeare pulsed out of Charlie with great clarity and beauty. He taught me about language all over again.

In the following years I would often go over to swim on summer afternoons when Charlie was preparing to direct or appear in *Major Barbara, The Apple Cart,* or, at Stratford-on-

Avon, *King Lear*. Charlie would float enormously about his pool, glad for my company, for I was silent, and he loved to talk theater and work out his ideas on character and style on anyone who had the good sense to listen.

It was the best school I ever had, and the best teacher.

I have not forgotten dear Charles Laughton's lessons.

Anything of mine you see on stage in the coming years will be touched by Charlie's presence. And, just at his elbow, Blackstone.

Their shared theater magic is very similar. What Laughton accomplished with language, Blackstone accomplished with conniption-fit machineries and illusory contraptions.

The two come together and fuse in my science-fiction plays *The Veldt* and *To the Chicago Abyss*.

Science fiction is what happened to magic when it passed through the hands of the alchemists and became future history. Somewhere along the line we changed caps, labels, and became more practical, but the effect is the same. Television is no less magical for being capable of explanation. I still don't believe it works. Airplanes don't fly; the laws are all wrong.

Our modern technologies, then, are the equivalents of old astrological frauds, alchemical lies, and the nightmares of prehistory. We must build the old terrors up in metal forms and steam them to stranger destinations, first in our psyches, and very soon after in three dimensions, two of which are more often than not surprise and horror. The third is, of course, delight. We wouldn't build these immense toys if we didn't dearly love to wind them up and let them run to Doom's End or Eternal Life, sometimes one, sometimes t'other.

I wrote *The Veldt* because my subconscious knew more about children than has often been told. It began as a word-association test, the sort of thing I often do mornings when I go from bed to my typewriter and let anything jump out on the page that wishes to jump. I wrote the word "nursery" on a piece of paper. I thought to myself, Past? No, Present? No, Future? Yes! A nursery in the future, what would it be like? Two hours later the lions were feeding on the far veldt in the last light of day, the work was done, I wrote *Finis* and stopped.

To the Chicago Abyss was written because sociologists, amateur and professional psychologists, and grand intellectual thinkers bore, distract, or irritate me to madness. I do not believe, and never have believed, that mediocrities hurt people. I have loved all the mass media, looked down on by the intelligentsia, as I grew up. I wanted to do a play about a man who could not recall great quality but only quantity, and that of such dumb stuffs as to be beneath consideration. The boy in me remembered Clark Bars and their bright circus wrappings, and I was off!

To the Chicago Abyss was written long years before Pop Art came on the scene. The story and the play proved to be more than a little prophetic. Since that time, also, motion pictures, once disdained, have been discovered to be an art form. Where was everyone forty years ago? How come I knew it when I was ten? To the Chicago Abyss says: Enjoy! If we took all of the junk out of life, our juices would dry up, the sap would go dead in the trees, we would occupy an intellectual graveyard and read each other's headstones.

The Wonderful Ice Cream Suit came out of my experiences as a child and young man in Roswell, New Mexico, Tucson, Arizona, and Los Angeles. I grew up with many boys of mixed Mexican-American blood. My best friend at junior high school was a boy named Eddie Barrera. When I was twenty-one I lived in and around a tenement at the corner of Figueroa Street and Temple in L.A., where, for five years, I saw my friends coming and going from Mexico City, Laredo, and Juarez. Their poverty and mine were identical. I knew what a suit could mean to them. I saw them share clothes, as I did with my father and brother. I remembered graduating from Los Angeles High School wearing a hand-me-down suit in which one of my uncles had been killed by a holdup man. There was a bullet hole in the front and one going out the back of the suit. My family was on government relief when I graduated. What else, then, but wear the suit, bullet holes and all?

So much for the genesis of these plays. Now, how does one produce them?

As simply as possible.

Let the Shakespearean and Oriental theater teach you. Little scenery, few props, and an immense enthusiasm for myth, metaphor, language to win the day.

In a science-fiction play, the harder you try to create the world of the future, the worse your failure. Simplicity was the keynote for our sets and costumes. In The Veldt, the various living areas of the future house were defined by nothing more than complex geometric patterns of bright nylon and other synthetic threads. The house looked very much like a fragile tapestry works. You could easily see through all the walls. The main door leading into the playroom-nursery was a spider-web like device which could expand or contract when pulled or released by other bright twines. Another minor psychological factor might be mentioned here; your average scrim, utilized in thousands of plays over the years, comes between your actors and the audience as an irritating obstruction. Our use of bright threads and twines was a good discovery. The audience never felt kept off, away, or obstructed, yet the feeling of a wall was there when we needed it.

When I first wrote *The Veldt* as a play, I had intended to project actual films of lions on a vast screen. This would have been an error of such immensity I can hardly believe I once entertained the idea.

Instead, I fell back on the lessons so amiably taught me by friend Laughton: stand in the center of the stage and create with words that world, these concepts, those carnivorous beasts.

The audience, then, was to become the veldt, and the sun-blazed lions. When in the playroom, my actors stared out and around in the wilderness that the audience became. This approach worked splendidly.

It worked also because we used sound tapes broadcast from the four corners of the auditorium. This allowed us to prowl the lion roars in circles around about and behind the audience, always keeping them a bit off-balance, never knowing where the sound of the lions might rise again in the long grass.

So I rediscovered an ancient fact. A well-written, well-spoken line creates more images than all the movies of the world. The Chinese were wrong. One word is worth a thousand pictures.

There are more than forty-two sound cues in *The Veldt*, and as many or more light cues.

This means you must find a stage manager, a lighting man, and a sound man of absolutely sterling quality, not liable to panics. The slightest error can throw *The Veldt* off-balance, drive the actors out of their minds, and send the director off to the nearest pub for the rest of the night.

Therefore, the technical rehearsals on *The Veldt* must be exhausting. This means staying up long after midnight in the final days before your opening to make sure that sound, light, and actors function as one whole. Your actors must sense each sound and light cue with hairline accuracy, so as to be able to relax and react truly to Africa "out beyond," hidden among the paying customers.

Every community has its hi-fi superconcussive sound nut. Find yours. Hire him. How? Lurk around your local woofer-tweeter outlet store. The guy with his hair standing on end, with a blind gaze and a bottle of ear medicine in his hand, is the expert at weird auditory hallucinations. Put up with him.

Trust him. He will gladly run you up a sound tape of electronic moans, groans, and future musics as will fill the bill for *The Veldt,* and *To the Chicago Abyss!* Ignore the fact that he belongs to a motorcycle gang and is an astrology freak. You can't have everything. Right now, the world of the future can be juiced into existence by superkinks such as he. I have had three tapes invented by a variety of unwashed technicians. All have been amazing. All have been of fine good use in providing yet one more element for our future plays.

In putting together your sound tape for *The Veldt,* your technician should be the next thing to an electronic composer. The scene where George commands the playroom to build him Egypt, the Pyramids, the Sphinx, Paris at the blue hour, etc., must be electronically orchestrated so we *hear* those things being reared up out of the earth into the sky, surrounding the audience with the sounds of electric creation.

Of course, if you are in high school or junior high school, lacking the hi-fi freak in the student body, search for some faculty member whose wig is permanently frazzled from too many hi's and not enough bass. Every school has one. Flatter him by asking for his help. And when in doubt, simplicity is the answer here, also. A few bits of electronic sound and some really good lion roars will save *The Veldt.*

We have spoken at length about *The Veldt.* Now, let us move on to *To the Chicago Abyss* and *The Wonderful Ice Cream Suit.*

In both of these plays we used magic lantern projections, immense photographic cels tossed up on scrims behind the actors to indicate changes of scene.

My good friend Joe Mugnaini, who has illustrated many of my books during the last nineteen years, painted a series of futuristic sets which we projected in images roughly ten to fifteen feet tall, enabling us to shift scenes, change locales, in two or three seconds flat. The six young men pursuing life in their Ice Cream Suit were thus able to race from street to suit emporium to apartment to Red Rooster Cafe with no long mood-shattering pauses for set-movers to strike and rebuild.

Similarly, in *To the Chicago Abyss,* my Old Man who remembered mediocrities could amble from park to interior apartment to night train, crossing empty midnight country in the merest breath of time, because of our illustrated projections.

Joe Mugnaini painted us the whole interior apartment house in skeletal outline so one could x-ray up through floor levels at hundreds of rooms, empty of furniture, haunted by lonely people. At the play's finale, he painted a cel on which were lumped and crammed the crowds of sleeping shadow people surrounding the Old Man on the late-night passenger train.

The inhabitants of the Ice Cream Suit live in a needed world of fantasy woven for them by the suit. The Old Man on his way to Chicago Abyss lives in his memories. Projected backgrounds, then, add yet another proper, right element to the people in these plays, immersed in dreams or half-dreams.

A minor but important detail. The scene in the Red Rooster Cafe where Toro grabs the Ice Cream Suit with Vamenos inside it must be played in SLOW MOTION, as indicated. This was an idea of Charles Rome Smith's which came to him during rehearsals. It proved to be beautiful in execution, enabling the audience to savor every small part of this major encounter, the terror and despair of all the young men surrounding Toro, trying to get him to let go of the suit, the bravery of Gomez coming back again and again to say "Hit me, not him," and being clouted for his trouble. All, all in the slowest motion, so we can see and hear every special instant up to the beautiful moment when Toro, struck on the head, slowly debates whether to accept unconsciousness, then, like an avalanche, subsides to the floor.

You are not going to be able to find six actors all with the same "skeletons" as Gomez puts it. So I dread to tell you the news, but you must have three or four or perhaps even five suits made and ready for the members of your cast, for the proper fit, and for the quick changes demanded by the scenes. We had five suits, which had to be cleaned two or three times a week. Luckily, our cleaner liked the play, and gave us rates!

Here, then, are the first three plays I wrote for my Pandemonium Theatre Company. Why such a company name? Because it pleased and delighted me. Because it was an unexpected and frivolous name to give a company of glad fools. And because it meant when you came into our theater, you never knew what special kind of hell might break loose.

Now . . .
Let the lions run.
Let the old man talk:
The Pandemonium Theatre Company,
from here on, is yours.

Ray Bradbury
Los Angeles
August 22, 1971

The Wonderful Ice Cream Suit

Production Note: The simpler the sets the better. The scrim that represents the "city" should give way easily to the poolroom, which is no more than a pool table, a chair, a light, and a scales. The clothing store could easily be nothing more nor less than a collection of men's dummies, with perhaps one small display case, a tie rack, and a mirror. The white suit itself could be enclosed in a curtained area to one side, and from it the "light" of the wonderful suit would emanate. The tenement room would be cots placed in a rough quadrangle. The bar would be a line of stools and some neon beer signs in the dark. The props should be everything: bright objects against dark backgrounds.

As the curtain rises, we see:

A lamppost in front of a café, a poolroom, a tenement. Three men lounge in various attitudes, enjoying the evening air. A jukebox is playing faintly somewhere. The three men seem to be waiting for something. They look here, they look there. Then:

A stranger walks briskly through. He drags on a cigarette, throws it over his shoulder as he exits.

The cigarette makes a lovely arc of fire in the air, lands on the sidewalk, but is there only a moment when it is retrieved by Villanazul, perhaps the oldest of the six men we will meet whose lives are joined in this summer evening. Villanazul is our dreamer-philosopher, but his movements are swiftly practical for all that.

He lifts the cigarette high and comes back, exhibiting it to the others.

VILLANAZUL

A meteor falls from space! It
leaves a path of fire in the dark.
It lands among us. It changes
our lives.

He takes a deep puff, passes it to Vamenos, the dirty one,
who sucks at it greedily. The third man, Martinez, has
to seize it away from him. He takes a leisurely puff, hands
it back to Villanazul. Then, together, the three men turn,
look at the sky, the city, and exhale a soft breath of cigarette smoke.

ALL

Ahhhhh . . .

MARTINEZ

It's a swell night, huh?

VAMENOS

Sure.

VILLANAZUL

Feel that silence. Ain't that a
fine silence. A man can think now.
A man can dream—

VAMENOS

(*puzzled but impressed*)
Hey . . . sure.

VILLANAZUL

In such weather as this—revolutions
occur.

MARTINEZ

Nights like this you wish—lots of
things.

VILLANAZUL

Thinking, I approve. Wishing however

is the useless pastime of the
unemployed.

VAMENOS
(*snorts*)
Unemployed, listen to him! We *got
no jobs*!

MARTINEZ
So we got no money, no friends.

VILLANAZUL
You, Martinez, have us. The friendship
of the poor is *real* friendship.

MARTINEZ
Yeah but . . .

Martinez stops, stares. The others stare with him. A handsome young Mexican with a fine thin moustache strolls
by, a woman on each careless arm, laughing. A guitar
plays beautifully as they pass. When they are gone, the
guitar goes, fading, with them.

MARTINEZ
(*slaps his brow*)
Madre mia, no! Two! How does he rate
two friends?!

VILLANAZUL
Such friendships are easily come by.
Economics, *compadre*.

VAMENOS
(*chews his black fingernail*)
He means—that guy's got a nice brand-new
summer suit. Looks sharp.

MARTINEZ
(*watching the people go by*)
Sure. And how am I dressed? Eh? Who

looks at me? There! In the tenement.
You see her?
(*points*)
In the fourth-floor window, the beautiful
girl leaning out? The long dark hair.
She's been there forever. That is to say,
six weeks. I have nodded, I have
smiled, I have blinked rapidly, I
have even bowed to her, on the street,
in the hall when visiting friends,
in the park, downtown. Even now,
look, I raise my hand, I move my
fingers, I wave to her. And what
happens—?

The others look, with Martinez, up and off in the air, waiting. Martinez lets his hand fall at last. They all slump.

VAMENOS

Nothing.

MARTINEZ

And more than nothing! *Madre mia!*
If just I had one suit! One! I
wouldn't need money, if I *looked OK* . . .

VILLANAZUL

I hesitate to suggest that you see
Gomez. But he's been talking some
crazy talk for a month now about
clothes. I keep on saying I'll be
in on it to make him go away. That
Gomez.

Another man has arrived, quietly, behind them.

THE MAN

Someone calls my name?

ALL

(*turning*)
Gomez!

GOMEZ

(*smiling*)
That's me.

VILLANAZUL

Gomez, show Martinez what you got in
your pocket!

GOMEZ

This?

Smiling, he pulls forth a long yellow ribbon which flutters
in the air.

MARTINEZ

(*blinking*)
Hey, what you doing with a tape
measure?

GOMEZ

(*proudly*)
Measuring people's skeletons.

MARTINEZ

Skeletons?

Gomez squints at Martinez and snaps his fingers.

GOMEZ

Caramba! Where you been all my life?
Let's try *you!*

He measures Martinez's arm, his leg, his chest. Martinez,
uncomfortable, tries to fend him off.

GOMEZ

Hold still! Chest—perfect!

Arm length—*perfectamente!*
The waist! Ah! Now—the height.
Turn around! Hold still!

Martinez turns. Gomez measures him from foot to crown.

GOMEZ

Five foot five! You're in. Shake
hands!

MARTINEZ

(*shaking hands, blankly*)
What have I done?

GOMEZ

You fit the measurements!
(*he stops*)
You got ten bucks?

VAMENOS

(*pulling out money*)
I got ten bucks! *I* want a suit!
Gomez, measure *me!*

GOMEZ

(*shunning Vamenos*)
Andale! Andale!

MARTINEZ

(*in awe*)
I got just nine dollars and 92 cents.
That'll buy a new suit? How come?
Why?

GOMEZ

Because you got the right skeleton.

MARTINEZ

(*pulling back*)
Mr. Gomez, I don't hardly know you—

GOMEN

GOMEZ

Know me? You are going to *live* with
me! Come on!

Gomez rushes through the poolroom door. The poolroom
lights flash on to show us no more than one pooltable,
a hanging overhead light, one chair, perhaps, and a weight
scales to one side. Reluctantly, Martinez is pushed into
the poolroom by a quietly competent Villanazul and an
eager and fawning Vamenos. Two men, Manulo and Dominguez, look up from their game of pool as Gomez waves
wildly at them.

GOMEZ

Manulo! Dominguez! The long search
has ended!

MANULO

(*drinks from wine bottle*)
Don't bother him. He has a most
important shot.

All stare as Dominguez uses his cue; the balls roll. They
click. Everyone is happy. Gomez leaps in.

GOMEZ

Dominguez, we have our fifth volunteer!

Dominguez has tabled his cue and taken out a little book.

DOMINGUEZ

The game is done. The game begins.
In my little black book here I have
a list of names of happy women who—
(*he breaks off*)
Caramba! Gomez! You mean—?

GOMEZ

Yes! Your money! Now! *Andale!*

Dominguez is torn between his little book and his news. Manulo is torn between his wine bottle and the news. Finally Dominguez puts the book down, takes some rumpled money from his pocket, looks at it, throws it on the green table. Reluctantly, Manulo does the same. Villanazul imitates them, once cynical, but caught up at last now, in the excitement.

GOMEZ
Ten! Twenty! Thirty!

They look to Martinez who, disconcerted, nevertheless counts out his bills and change. To which Gomez adds his own money, lifting all the cash like a royal flush, waving it.

GOMEZ
Forty! Fifty bucks! The suit costs
sixty! All we need is ten bucks!

VILLANAZUL
And the sooner the better, Gomez.
That wonderful ice-cream suit won't
last forever. I seen people looking
at it in the suit-store window. Only
one of a kind! We got to hurry.

MARTINEZ
Wait there, hey! *The* suit? *Uno?*
(*holds up one finger*)

GOMEZ
(*does likewise*)
Uno. One.

MARTINEZ
Ice cream . . . ?

GOMEZ
White. White as vanilla ice cream,
white white like the summer moon!

MARTINEZ

But who gets to own this one suit?

VILLANAZUL, MANULO, and DOMINGUEZ
(*quickly, smiling, one after another*)
Me. Me. Me.

GOMEZ

Me. And *you!* OK, guys, line up!

Villanazul, Manulo, Dominguez rush to put their backs to the poolroom wall. Gomez lines up with them, fourth in line, and snaps a command at Martinez.

GOMEZ

Martinez, the other end!

Martinez takes his place at the other end of the line.

GOMEZ

Vamenos, lay that billiard cue
across the tops of our heads!

VAMENOS

(*eagerly*)
Sure, sure, sure!

Vamenos places the cue across the tops of the five men's heads, moving along. The cue lies flat and without a rise or fall. Martinez leans out to see what is happening and is stunned with revelation.

MARTINEZ

Ah! Ah!

Gomez turns his head to smile down the line at Martinez.

GOMEZ

You see!

The men are laughing now, happy with this trick.

MARTINEZ

We're *all* the same *height!*

ALL

(*laughing almost drunkenly*)
Sure! Sure! The same!

Gomez runs down the line with his tape measure, rustling it about the men so they laugh even more.

GOMEZ

Sure! It took a month, four weeks,
to find four guys the same size and
shape as me, a month of running
around, measuring. Sometimes I found
guys with five-foot-five skeletons,
sure, but all the meat on their bones
was too much or not enough. Sometimes
their bones were too long in the legs
or too short in the arms. Boy, all
the bones! But now, five of us, same
shoulders, chests, waists, arms, and
as for the *weight?* Men!
(*points*)

The men march onto the weight scales, one after another. Vamenos, eager to be of service to his gods, puts in a penny for each. The machine grinds and lets drop for each a tiny card which he holds up to peer at, to read aloud, to announce proudly.

MANULO

144 pounds!

He steps down, Dominguez steps up. The penny drops. The machine grinds. The new card falls out into his hands.

DOMINGUEZ

146!

Villanazul is next, and reads out:

VILLANAZUL

(*quietly proud*)

142.

Gomez weighs himself.

GOMEZ

145!

He waves Martinez aboard. Martinez shouts the result.

MARTINEZ

144! A miracle!!

VILLANAZUL

(*simply*)

No . . . Gomez.

They all smile upon Gomez, the saint. who puts his arms about them, circling them in. Vamenos hovers in the background, pretending to be part of all this.

GOMEZ

Are we not fine? All the same size.
All the same dream: the suit. So
each of us will look beautiful, eh,
at least one night every week!

MARTINEZ

I haven't looked beautiful in years.
The girls run away.

GOMEZ

They will run no more, they will
freeze, when they see you in the
cool white summer ice-cream suit.

VILLANAZUL

Gomez, just tell me one thing.

GOMEZ

Of course, *compadre*.

VILLANAZUL

When we get this nice new white ice-
cream summer suit, some night you
won't put it on and walk down to the
Greyhound bus in it and go live in
El Paso for a year in it, will you?

GOMEZ

Villanazul, how can you *say* that?

VILLANAZUL

My eye sees and my tongue moves.
How about the EVERYBODY WINS! punch-
board lotteries you ran and kept
running when nobody won? How about
the United Chili con Carne and
Frijole Company you were going to
organize and all that ever happened
was the rent ran out on a two-by-four
office?

GOMEZ

The errors of a child, now grown!
Enough! In this hot weather, someone
may buy the special suit that is made
just for us that stands waiting in
the window of Shumway's Sunshine Suits!
We have fifty dollars. Now we need
just one more skeleton!

Everyone tries not to notice Vamenos, twitching nearby.

VAMENOS

Me! My skeleton! Measure it! It's
great! Sure, my hands are big, and

my arms, from digging ditches—
but—

As he talks, he grabs the tape and measures himself. His plea is falling on dull ears until, outside, we hear the guitar, the man and his two women passing, laughing. At this, anguish moves over the faces of the five men in the poolroom, like the shadow of a summer cloud. It is too much for them. They wish to weep. They turn again, in agony, to examine Vamenos. Not daring to speak, Vamenos runs over to the penny scale and nervously drops in a penny. The machine grinds. The white card flips into the slot below. Vamenos, eyes closed, breathes a prayer.

VAMENOS
Madre mia . . . Please.

He opens his eyes and looks at the card.

VAMENOS
145 pounds! Another miracle!
Isn't it? Eh?
    (*pauses*)
Eh . . . ?

He turns and holds out the card for them in one hand, his ten-dollar bill in the other.

The men look at him, for a long time, sweating.

Gomez breaks, snatches the ten-dollar bill.

GOMEZ
The clothing store! *Andale!* The suit!
The suit!

Vamenos lets out a battle yell of delight. All rush out. Martinez hesitates, shaking his head.

MARTINEZ
Santos, what a dream. White as the

summer moon, he said. Six men. One
suit. What will come of this? Madness?
Debauchery? Murder? But then—I go
with God. He will protect me.

Martinez, seeing that the others are gone, runs, but stops,
sees something on the table, grabs it.

MARTINEZ
Hey, Dominguez! You left your black
book with the kind ladies' names!
Dominguez! Hey! Hey!
   (*exits*)

Blackout.

In the darkness, the guitar music is very loud and fast.
To it, we hear the sound of their running feet. At last,
it all fades away as . . . the lights come up again and
we see. . .

A neon light flashes: SHUMWAY'S SUNSHINE SUIT
SHOP.

Here and there are male mannequins displaying the very
niftiest men's fashions. These, and a few racks of shoes
and ties, are the furniture of Shumway's. To one side is
a green curtained booth, the curtains pulled.

Mr. Shumway and his assistant, Leo, enter, bringing a new
shipment of ties.

MR. SHUMWAY
Bring the ties, Leo.

LEO
A pleasure, Mr. Shumway. Such fine
ties. Look.

MR. SHUMWAY
I looked, Leo.

                    LEO
Feel. I . . .

Leo stops, surprised, because Gomez has just popped in
through the front door, popped out again, casually, hands
in pockets.

Mr. Shumway has not seen this.

                 MR. SHUMWAY
Something wrong, Leo?

                    LEO
Nothing, Mr. Shumway.
    (*turns away*)

                 MR. SHUMWAY
Like I said—

Now, Mr. Shumway has caught a fleeting glimpse. Villanazul this time, strolling in from the dark, peers around,
worried, strolls out.

                    LEO
Something wrong, Mr. Shumway?

                 MR. SHUMWAY
It's too early to tell, Leo.

They go on racking the ties. Next time, both Mr. Shumway and Leo turn just as Martinez and Manulo dart by.

                    LEO
    (*stunned*)
Two this time.

                 MR. SHUMWAY
    (*getting suspicious*)
It couldn't be—a gang is planning
to rob my store . . . ?

                              LEO
Rob . . . ?

At which point, Vamenos, alone, appears in the doorway,
exhaling smoke, puffing on his villainous cigar, looking
thoroughly disreputable, unshaven, and fly-specked.

Leo and Mr. Shumway are riven by the image, which after
inspecting the shop casually, wanders off, dropping ashes,
into the night. Shumway panics, shoving an object at Leo.

                         MR. SHUMWAY
          Leo, hide this in the suit on the
          dummy!

                              LEO
          Your *wallet!*

Leo does not move—so, panicking, Mr. Shumway thrusts
the wallet into the dummy's inside pocket, just in time,
for all *six* of the men have drifted into the doorway.

Feeling their presence, Mr. Shumway pretends to fix the
dummy's tie.

                          SHUMWAY
          The telephone, Leo. Pretend you're
          making just a call . . . the police . . .

Leo edges toward the phone. As he picks it up. Gomez
cries out.

                           GOMEZ
          It's gone!

                          SHUMWAY
          Quick, Leo! The police!

                         VILLANAZUL
          The police? Hey, wait!

All six men rush forward.

GOMEZ

Where is it? Where!?

SHUMWAY

(*points*)
The money!? The inside
pocket!

GOMEZ

Money?

VAMENOS

No, no! The *suit!*

SHUMWAY

The suit . . . ?

All the men freeze like statues, waiting for Gomez to give
tongue to their fear.

GOMEZ

You . . . didn't . . . *sell* it?

SHUMWAY

(*puzzled*)
I didn't?

LEO

What didn't Mr. Shumway sell?

VAMENOS

The only suit in the world!

MANULO

The ice-cream white!

GOMEZ

Size thirty-four!

MARTINEZ

Was in your window just an hour ago!

LEO

(*exhaling*)
That suit?

SHUMWAY

(*in disbelief*)
That's what you want?
(*almost hysterical with relief*)
Leo . . . ?

LEO

The booth?

SHUMWAY

(*eyes closed*)
The booth.

Everyone watches as Shumway, like a pontiff, leads the
way. Leo is ahead of him and takes hold of the green
curtains on the front of the booth. Shumway turns, totally
relaxed at last, and glances eagerly about.

SHUMWAY

For which gentleman?

GOMEZ

All of us.

SHUMWAY

(*dismayed again*)
All?

MARTINEZ

All for one! One for all!

The phrase proves felicitous. The crowd mills about happily, pounding Martinez on the back, proud of his creative
rhetoric.

THE CROWD

Sure! Hey! Great! All! All!

Shumway, undaunted, pontifically accepting this freshly batted shuttlecock of fate, nods to them, then briskly to Leo. Leo sweeps back the curtain. Shumway seizes a light cord, jerks it, points in.

SHUMWAY

Gents. There she is. The 59-
dollar, 59-cent pure
white vanilla ice-cream summer
suit!

The men stare, riven. We cannot see into the booth. We only see the reflected pure white, holy light of the suit shimmering out like illumination from some far Arctic floe. The men's faces are washed in snowy color. They peer in as at a shrine.

ALL

Ahhhhhhh . . .

LEO

(*sotto voce*)
Mr. Shumway . . . *one* suit? Ain't that
a dangerous precedent to set? What
if *everyone* bought suits this way?

ALL

(*murmuring*)
Ah . . . ah . . .

Shumway puts his hand on Leo's shoulder like a father. He nods to the wondrous crowd of men.

SHUMWAY

Listen. You ever *hear* one 59-
dollar suit make so many
people happy at one time?

The six men, their faces glowing with the suit's reflection, still peer, smiling, into the booth.

> VAMENOS
>
> White ... so white it puts out my
> eyes!
> (*he squints*)

> MARTINEZ
>
> White as angel's wings ...

Mr. Shumway and Leo peer over the six men's backs and nod, proudly.

> SHUMWAY
>
> You know something, Leo? That's a
> *suit!*

Blackout.

Music.

We hear the six men's voices yelling, singing, shouting. They reenter and pass before the drawn curtain or dark scrim on their way to the tenement.

> GOMEZ
>
> (*points ahead*)
> There's my place! You all move in
> with me. Save money on rent as well
> as clothes. Martinez, you got the
> suit?

Enter, Martinez, surrounded by helpers, a white gift box among them.

> MARTINEZ
>
> Have I! From *us* to *us!* Aye-yah!

> GOMEZ
>
> Who's got the dummy?

Vamenos, chewing his cigar, waltzes in, scattering sparks, clutching a headless clothes dummy.

VAMENOS
Who else! Watch *us!*

At which point, Vamenos slips. The dummy falls. Pandemonium. Everyone yells. Vamenos retrieves the dummy, sheepishly.

VAMENOS
(*to himself*)
Vamenos, you clumsy! Idiot!

They seize the dummy from him. To retrieve himself, Vamenos snaps his fingers.

VAMENOS
Hey, we got to celebrate! I'll
go borrow some wine!

He almost falls, scattering sparks, as he runs. The others peer after him.

GOMEZ
(*unhappily*)
All right, guys, inside. Break
out the suit!

The others hurry off, leaving Martinez with Gomez.

MARTINEZ
Hey, Gomez, you look sick.

GOMEZ
I am. What have I *done?*

He waves toward the others.

GOMEZ
I pick Manulo, a great man with

the guitar. I pick Dominguez, a
fiend, a devil with the women, but
who sings sweet, eh? So far so
good. I pick Villanazul who reads
books.

MARTINEZ
I like to hear him talk.

GOMEZ
I pick you, you wash behind your
ears. But *then* what do I do? Can
I wait? No! I got to buy that
suit! So the last man I pick is
a clumsy slob who has the right to
wear my suit—*our* suit—one night
a week! Maybe to fall downstairs
in it, burn it—Why, why did I *do*
it!

Martinez starts to speak when Villanazul calls from off
right, softly, lovingly.

VILLANAZUL
Gomez, the suit is ready!

MARTINEZ
Let's go see if it looks as good
in *your* apartment with *your* light
bulb.

They run off.

Blackout.

When the lights rise again we find ourselves in the tenement apartment with three of the men clustered around
an unseen object. Gomez and Martinez enter from a door
to the right rear. Gomez only half-looks at the working
men.

GOMEZ

Ready?

VILLANAZUL

Almost!

Gomez turns away, eyes shut.

GOMEZ

Is it on the dummy?

MANULO

Almost!

They make half-hidden adjustments.

GOMEZ

Just the one light, overhead!

Martinez scurries to shut off various lamps.

VILLANAZUL

There!

MANULO

You can look now.

VILLANAZUL

(softly)
Gomez...

Gomez turns. They stand aside. Martinez turns on the overhead light. There, as Gomez opens his eyes, is the phosphorescent, the miraculous white suit, shimmering like a ghost among them. None dare touch, but move in awe around it.

GOMEZ

(exhales)
Madre mia...!

MARTINEZ

(whispering)
It's even better!

MANULO
... White ... as clouds ... on a summer
night ...

GOMEZ
... Like the milk in the bottles in
the halls at dawn ...

Villanazul, his face reflecting the whiteness of the suit,
speaks.

VILLANAZUL
White ... white as the snow on the
mountain near our town in Mexico
called the Sleeping Lady ...

The others nod.

GOMEZ
(*quietly*)
Say that again, please.

Villanazul, proud yet humble, is glad to repeat his tribute.

VILLANAZUL
... White as the snow on the mountain
called ...

Smoke is exhaled about all their faces from one side.
Slowly, all of them turn to see who is there. Vamenos,
smiling, is behind them, smoking, holding a wine bottle up.

VAMENOS
I'm back! A party! The wine!
Eh, who gets to wear the suit
first tonight! Me?

GOMEZ
(*panicky; peers at watch*)
It's too late. Nine o'clock!

VAMENOS

(*shocked*)
Late!

ALL

Late?!!

Dominguez goes to the window to look, to point down.

DOMINGUEZ

(*to music*)
Late? It is a fine Saturday night
in a summer month. The air is sweet.
Hear the far music? While women
drift through the warm darkness
like flowers on a quiet stream . . .

The men make a mournful, trapped sound. The far guitar
dies.

VILLANAZUL

(*wielding pad and pencil*)
Gomez, I ask the favor. You wear
the suit tonight from nine-thirty
to ten. Manulo till ten-thirty,
Dominguez till eleven, myself till
eleven-thirty, Martinez till midnight—

VAMENOS

(*indignant; removing cigar from mouth*)
Hey! Why me *last?*

MARTINEZ

(*thinking quickly*)
After midnight is the best time of
all!

VAMENOS

(*thinks*)
Sure. That's *right!*

(*smiles*)
OK.

GOMEZ

OK. And from tonight on, we each
wear the suit one night a week, eh?
On the extra night, Sunday, we draw
straws to see who wears the suit then.

VAMENOS

Me, *every* time! I'm *lucky!*

Every face falls at this news.

MANULO

Can the talk! Gomez, you thought
of this. You wear the suit first!

Gomez manages to tear his eyes away from the disreputable Vamenos. He accepts fate and shrugs. Then, impulsively, like a snake shedding his skin in one great move-
ment, he shucks off his old coat and shirt, almost in one
motion, yelling.

GOMEZ

Aye-hah! Aye-yeeeeeeee!

Blackout.

Fast guitar.

In the dark, more happy cries: "The clean shirt!" "Here!"
"The pants!" "Here!" "Now the new socks!" "The socks!"
"Who ties the best tie?" "Me!" "The shoes!" "All pol-
ished!" "Now, now—at last—The coat if you please!"

The lights come up. The men are gathered, we think, to
the dummy, as before, fussing with it. Then they stand
back.

Gomez stands alone in the center of their excitement.

VILLANAZUL

Ah!

MANULO

Gomez, you look like a saint!
  (*looks up*)
Forgive me, God, for saying that!

Gomez is like a bullfighter posed there, imperturbably proud, waiting for the last investment with his "suit of lights." He gestures. Villanazul and Martinez together lift the coat behind him.

VILLANAZUL and MARTINEZ

The coat! Here!

GOMEZ

  (*breathes in*)
Oh, it even smells good!

VILLANAZUL

How clean it sounds! Listen!
How easily it whispers, going on!

They all listen as Gomez assumes the sleeves. He poses like a matador! Far away, a loving crowd sighs: "Ole!"

GOMEZ

  (*after the beat*)
We got no mirror!

VILLANAZUL

Sure you got a mirror! Here.
All of us! Stand close.

Villanazul arranges the others close-packed with himself. Gomez falls in with this kindness, and preens himself before them. They look where he walks, turns, adjusts his tie, fixes his cuff. Their gaze is bright.

GOMEZ

Ah, God, I can see myself in your

eyes, your faces! Put me in a
store window, I don't deserve to
go out!

VILLANAZUL
(*softly*)
Out, Gomez ... out ...

He smiles into that "mirror" and goes to the door, where
he places his ears, eyes shut.

GOMEZ
Listen to all those women out there
... waiting.

They listen. They nod. Gomez turns about once and goes
out left. As the door slams,

Blackout.

Guitar music.

Then, almost immediately, Gomez reenters far stage left.

The tenement room is, of course, gone. A spotlight fixes
Gomez as he adjusts his tie and checks the button on his
coat and lovingly touches the snowy sleeves of the suit.
Then he looks up and out.

A voice speaks from the darkness!

THE VOICE
Gomez! Is that you?!

He looks left.

In a spotlight, hanging upon the air is a long, semitrans-
parent scarf hung floating, provocative, light, soft, beautiful.

GOMEZ
Rosita!

Another voice speaks from further over.

THE SECOND VOICE
Gomez! I didn't know you!

A second spot flicks on. In it drifts a second long and diaphanous scarf, a different color. Gomez bows to it.

GOMEZ
Marguerita, it is me!

Other voices call. Other scarves appear in a double line across the darkness.

THE VOICES
Gomez! Gomez! Gomez!
Que hermosa! Where are you going?

GOMEZ
This way!

He runs. On the way, he "reaps" the scarves, a half dozen over his right arm, a half dozen over his left.

Blackout.

Music.

The lights come on again almost immediately to find the owners of the suit waiting on each side of the apartment door.

VAMENOS
Half hour's up!

MARTINEZ
Where's Gomez?

VILLANAZUL
Wait! Listen! He's outside the door.

They listen.

VAMENOS

Someone's out there, OK.

MARTINEZ

Why don't he come in?!

Villanazul opens the door. Gomez stands there, entranced with his experience with the suit, arms out away from his body as if a half dozen "women" were draped over each.

VILLANAZUL

Gomez! Come in! How was it?

Gomez wanders in. His arms are, of course, empty, but the memory of his encounters lingers. He dreams. He floats.

MARTINEZ

Gomez! *Say* something!

Gomez takes a deep breath, sighs, and says at last:

GOMEZ

Who's next?

MANULO

Me!

Manulo darts in from off right, stripped to his shorts. Everyone shouts.

Blackout.

Music.

When the light comes up, the music slows. Now who do we find but Manulo playing the guitar, a little louder, a little faster, luring from the shadows, with the whiteness of his suit and the playing of his music, the shapes of women, perhaps the two women whom we saw earlier passing on the arms of the stranger. The two women reach Manulo, who pretends not to see them drawn to him. At the last moment he strikes a chord, tosses the guitar aside, embraces them both. Blackout.

ALL

(*in darkness*)
Who's next? Dominguez!

Fast music. And the spotlight again. And dancing to the music, in the spotlight—in the white suit—Dominguez! He whirls about, he poses. Blackout.

ALL

(*in darkness*)
Who's next? Villanazul!

The music is very slow and thoughtful. Villanazul comes out of the darkness, looking here and there, all about. He is wearing the suit now and looks warmly happy. A single sign is posted: THE PLAZA. There is a vast muttering, murmuring, as of many people in a good argument. Villanazul moves like a fish in his proper element, bathed in the free flow of words. We can hear a few snatches of the discussions being carried on.

ONE VOICE

—there is only one way to stop the
gold from flowing out of the country—

A SECOND VOICE

—in the next election, as an individual,
I say to you people in the Plaza—we can
only look—

Villanazul has reached a small soapbox. He *ascends* it.

Almost immediately there is a hush, a different kind of murmur.

With a single proud but benevolent nod, Villanazul tunes down the murmur another decibel. With one smile he brings absolute cutoff silence. He waits a heartbeat and then:

VILLANAZUL
Friends. Do you know Thomas Carlyle's
book *Sartor Resartus?* In that book
we find *his* Philosophy of *Suits* . . . !!

The audience gasps in admiration.

The spot on Villanazul grows intensely bright.

The audience lets out its admiration in a great "Ah!" as
if watching a bright fireworks come down amongst them.

And as the "Ah" fades, so does the light.

Darkness.

And we hear a single chord of the guitar.

And then another.

And at last from a door on the far stage right, Martinez
ventures with great trepidation out, and moves through the
darkness to stand under a window to the far left.

MARTINEZ
This is where she lives. That is
her window. She *must* feel the
suit burning even through those
walls. Come on, suit! Bring her
to the window.

He shuts his eyes. He leans on the night, eagerly, thinking.
A small light comes on in the window above.

Martinez opens his eyes at this.

MARTINEZ
Yes!

A brighter light comes on.

MARTINEZ
Yes!

A shadow moves at the window.

MARTINEZ

Yes!

The window opens, the beautiful young woman is there.

MARTINEZ

(*softly*)
Yes.

The young woman looks around, as if she had been hearing her name called for some minutes and that is why she has come to the window.

MARTINEZ

(*whispers*)
This way.

The young woman looks off into the distance, a strange expression in her eyes.

MARTINEZ

(*as above*)
Here . . . !

But still she looks all around.

MARTINEZ

What's wrong?!! Ah, God, even
the *blind* can see this suit!

The girl looks down, squints.

MARTINEZ

Ah . . .

He starts to speak. The girl turns, vanishes.

MARTINEZ

(*stunned*)
No! No . . .

But now she returns. She lifts her hand. A pair of horn-rimmed glasses appear in that hand.

> MARTINEZ
> *Madre mia,* speak of the lovely
> blind . . .

She peers about then sees something.

> THE YOUNG WOMAN
> (*to herself*)
> What is that whiteness down there?

> MARTINEZ
> (*half aloud, an anxious whisper*)
> The suit! The suit!

> THE YOUNG WOMAN
> What is that *other* whiteness down
> there?

Martinez beams up, all teeth.

At last she puts on her glasses.

> THE YOUNG WOMAN
> A smile!

> MARTINEZ
> (*waves politely once, nods*)
> Manuel Martinez.

Shyly she looks down at him through her horn-rims.

> THE YOUNG WOMAN
> (*quietly*)
> Celia Obregon.

> MARTINEZ
> (*remembering it*)
> Celia Obregon.

THE YOUNG WOMAN

(*likewise*)
Manuel Martinez.

MARTINEZ

Next Wednesday night, may I
visit your family?

THE YOUNG WOMAN

Yes.

MARTINEZ

You will not forget?

She takes off her glasses.

THE YOUNG WOMAN

No. I see you clearly, even now.
The two whitenesses. The suit.
The smile.

MARTINEZ

I will bring them both!
Celia Obregon.

THE YOUNG WOMAN

Manuel Martinez.

She shuts the window. The light goes out.

Martinez crows like a rooster, happily turning in circles.

MARTINEZ

Aye-hah! Heeee! Oh, friends!
Gomez! Villanazul! Manulo!!
Dominguez! *To* you! *For* you!
With you!

He makes one fine pool shot as he names Gomez. He *rrr-rolls* the name of Villanazul. Shouting "Manulo!" and "Dominguez!" he strums a guitar once, twice, throws it into darkness, and furiously dances as the lights black out and the music continues in a fine frenzy.

As soon as possible the lights come on in the tenement room. The men are waiting by the door. Manulo is listening, his ear to the keyhole.

> MANULO
> *Atencion!* Here comes someone!
> Martinez! He's singing!

We hear the singing.

> MANULO
> He's dancing!

We hear the dancing, as do the coowners of the suit.

> MANULO
> He's drunk!

There is a knock on the door, one, two!

Villanazul opens the door. Martinez looks in, smiling.

> MARTINEZ
> I am looking for Manuel Martinez!

Everyone gasps, bemused, puzzled.

> VILLANAZUL
> Manuel, *you* are Martinez!

> MARTINEZ
> No, no! Martinez is gone! In his
> place—who knows?

> MANULO
> He's drunk!

> MARTINEZ
> With the *suit!* With *life!* Us all
> together! The store, here, and
> laughing, and feeling more drunk,

eh, without drinking, and everyone
in and out of the coat, the pants,
grabbing hold, falling, eh? And one
walking out and coming back, and
another, and another, and now *me!*
Here *I* am! So tall! So pure! Like
one who gives orders and the world
grows quiet and moves aside . . .
Martinez, who is he? Who am I?

DOMINGUEZ

Here! Look! We borrowed this while
you were out!

GOMEZ

Three mirrors, count them!

Manulo and Dominguez run forward carrying a three-way
mirror which they set up.

MARTINEZ

(*with delight*)
Ah! Ah! Look! Three men! Who are
they? There's Manulo! Inside the
suit! And Dominguez!

MANULO

Hey, what?

DOMINGUEZ

Let *me* see!

They crowd around. Manulo puts his head on Martinez's
left shoulder, posing. Dominguez puts his head on the
right shoulder. Martinez now has three heads.

MANULO and DOMINGUEZ

Ah! Ah!

MARTINEZ

And Gomez and Villanazul!

They crowd in, too, with general elation. Only Vamenos stands back, uneasily.

GOMEZ

There we *all* are!

VILLANAZUL

Don't we look good? Ah. Touch the
mirrors this way, that. See? In
the glass! A thousand, a million
Gomezes, Manulos, Dominguezes,
Martinezes, march off in white
armor, away down the line,
reflected, re-reflected again
and again, indomitable, forever!

MANULO

(*quietly*)
Don't he speak pretty? Villanazul,
you speak pretty.

Martinez takes off the coat. He holds it out on the air. In a trance, the others stand back as a dirty hand reaches to take the coat.

GOMEZ

Vamenos!

Martinez freezes. Vamenos pulls back his hand.

VAMENOS

(*blows smoke*)
What did *I* do?

GOMEZ

Fire eater! Pig! You didn't wash.
Or even shave!

ALL

(*seizing him*)
The bath! The bath!

VAMENOS

No, mercy! The night air!
My death and burial! No!

They hustle him as the lights go out. There is a furious
sound of thundering water, splashes, groans, the sound of
a body heaved in, Vamenos protesting. From darkness we
hear:

VAMENOS

I'm drowned!

GOMEZ

No! No! Just clean!

DOMINGUEZ

Where's the razor?

MANULO

Here!

VAMENOS

Cut my throat, it's quicker!

More water, more thunder, more shouts, and then at last
the plug pulled and the great suction away down in the
night. All fades to silence. The lights now come slowly
up. Five men are standing in a circle on one side of
the room, working over some unseen statue like careful
and exceptionally neat sculptors.

VILLANAZUL

There.

MANULO

I can't believe it.

DOMINGUEZ

It's him, all right.

MARTINEZ

(in awe)
Vamenos . . .

They move back, away, to reveal Vamenos, unbelievable
indeed in the white suite, his beard shaved, hair combed,
hands clean.

He goes to look in the mirror.

                              VAMENOS
   Is that *me?!*

                              VILLANAZUL
   That's Vamenos all right. Of whom
   it is said that when Vamenos walks
   by, avalanches itch on mountaintops,
   flea-maddened dogs dance about on
   their muddy paws, and locomotives
   belch forth their blackest soots to
   be lifted in flags to salute him.
   Ah, Vamenos, Vamenos, suddenly the
   world *sizzles* with flies. And here
   you are, a huge, fresh-frosted cake.

                              MANULO
      (*sadly*)
   You sure look keen in that suit,
   Vamenos.

                              VAMENOS
   Thanks.

He twitches uneasily under their stare, trying to make his
skeleton comfortable where all their skeletons have so re-
cently been. There is a long pause.

                              VAMENOS
      (*faintly*)
   Can I go now?

Another pause, in which Gomez suddenly cries:

                              GOMEZ
   Villanazul! A pencil! Paper!

VILLANAZUL
(*whipping them out*)
Okay!

GOMEZ
Copy down these rules for Vamenos.

VILLANAZUL
Ready.

GOMEZ
Rule number one.

VAMENOS
(*listening close*)
One, yes.

GOMEZ
Don't fall down in that suit.

VAMENOS
I won't.

GOMEZ
Two: don't lean against buildings
in that suit.

VAMENOS
No buildings.

GOMEZ
Don't walk under trees with birds
in them in that suit.

VILLANAZUL
(*writing*)
... birds ...

VAMENOS
(*eager to please*)
... trees, no, no trees.

MARTINEZ
(*chiming in*)
Don't smoke!

DOMINGUEZ
Don't drink!

GOMEZ
Good, no smokes, no drinks—

VAMENOS
(*cuts in*)
Please. Can I *sit down* in this suit?

VILLANAZUL
When in doubt—take the pants off,
fold them over a chair.

Everyone looks at the philosopher, pleased. Villanazul goes on, writing, pleased with himself.

Vamenos mops his brows with his handkerchief. He edges toward the door, gingerly.

VAMENOS
Well . . . wish me luck.

GOMEZ
(*a real prayer*)
Go with God, Vamenos.

ALL
Aye . . . aye . . .

He waves a little wave. He opens the door. He goes out quickly. He shuts it.

There is a ripping sound!

GOMEZ
Madre de dios!

All stand, riven by the terrible sound.

VILLANAZUL
Vamenos!

He whips the door open.

There stands Vamenos, two halves of a torn handkerchief in his hands.

> VAMENOS
>
> Rrrrip! Look at those faces!
> (*He tears the cloth again*)
> Rrrrip! Oh, oh, your faces! Ha!

Laughing, Vamenos slams the door, leaving them stunned. Gomez sinks slowly into a chair.

> GOMEZ
>
> Stone me! Kill me! I have sold
> our souls to a demon!

Villanazul digs in his pockets, takes out a coin.

> VILLANAZUL
>
> Here is my last 50 cents. Who
> else will help me buy back Vamenos'
> share of the suit?

> MANULO
> (*displaying a dime*)
> It's no use. We got only enough to
> buy the lapels and buttonholes.

At the window, Dominguez reports, looking down.

> DOMINGUEZ
>
> There goes Vamenos. He's in the
> street. Hey! Vamenos!
> (*leans out*)
> No!

Gomez leaps up.

> GOMEZ
>
> What's he doing?

DOMINGUEZ

Picking up a cigar butt and lighting
it . . .

Gomez tears to the window.

GOMEZ

Vamenos! Pig! No cigars! Away!

DOMINGUEZ

There. Ah.
    (*relaxes*)
Now he is making a very strange gesture
to us with his hand.
    (*waves*)
The same to you, friend. There he
goes.

GOMEZ

There goes our suit, you mean.

Everyone has drifted or hurried to the window now. They
are crushed together, worriedly, looking out and down.

MANULO

I bet he eats a hamburger in
that suit.

VILLANAZUL

I'm thinking of the mustard.

GOMEZ

    (*turns away; pained*)
Don't! No, no.

MANULO

I need a drink, bad.

MARTINEZ

Manulo, there's wine here, this
bottle—

But Manulo is out the door. It shuts.

Gomez stands alone with his thoughts. The others fidget. After a moment, Villanazul, with a great pretense of being casual, stretches, yawns, strolls toward the door.

> VILLANAZUL
> I think I'll just walk down to
> the plaza, friends.

Villanazul exits. The others look at the door, the window, the door, the window.

> GOMEZ
> Can you still see it?

> DOMINGUEZ
> (*at the window*)
> Who?

> GOMEZ
> The suit! And the monster in it!

> DOMINGUEZ
> He's a long way off there. He's
> turning down Hill Avenue. That's
> a dark street, ain't it?

> GOMEZ
> (*twitching*)
> How should I know!

Dominguez ambles toward the door. Gomez, his back turned, feels the motion.

> GOMEZ
> Dominguez?

> DOMINGUEZ
> (*guiltily takes his hands off the door*)
> Eh?

GOMEZ

If you just happen—

DOMINGUEZ

Eh?

GOMEZ

Hell, if you should bump into, run
into Vamenos, by accident, I mean,
warn him away from Mickey Murillo's
Red Rooster Café. They got fights
not only *on* but *out front* of the
TV, too, there.

MARTINEZ

Mickey Murillo's Red Rooster Café.
That's on Hill Avenue, right?

DOMINGUEZ

(*nervously*)
He wouldn't go into Murillo's.
That suit means too much to
Vamenos.

MARTINEZ

Sure.

DOMINGUEZ

He wouldn't do anything to hurt it.

GOMEZ

Sure.

DOMINGUEZ

He'd shoot his mother, first.

MARTINEZ

Any day.

DOMINGUEZ

Well . . .

GOMEZ and MARTINEZ

Well?

Dominguez takes the cue. He exits, fast.

Martinez and Gomez, alone, listen to Dominguez's foot-
steps hurry away downstairs. Now they circle the
undressed window dummy. Gomez returns at last to the
window, where he stands biting his lip and at last, unhappily, begins to search through his clothes until at last
from a pocket he draws forth a piece of pink folded paper.

GOMEZ

Martinez, take this.

MARTINEZ

What is it? Names. Numbers.
    (*reads*)
Hey! A ticket on the bus to
El Paso a week from now!

GOMEZ

    (*nods*)
Turn it in. Get the money.

MARTINEZ

You were going to El Paso, alone?

GOMEZ

No. With the suit.
    (*a beat*)
But now, after tonight, I don't
know. Hell, I'm crazy. Turn it
in. We may need the money to buy
back Vamenos' share. With what's
left over, we buy a nice new white
Panama hat to go with the white
ice-cream suit, eh?

MARTINEZ

Gomez—

GOMEZ

Boy, is it hot in here! I need air.

MARTINEZ

Gomez. I am touched.

GOMEZ

Shut up. Maybe the white suit
don't even *exist* anymore.
Andale!

Gomez runs out. Martinez starts to follow, comes back,
pats the dummy for luck, reaches up, jerks the light string
—blackout. We hear the door slam as he leaves.

Fast guitar music.

In the darkness after a time, as the guitar confines itself
to single chords, a neon sign blinks on and off to the music: MICKEY MURILLO'S RED ROOSTER CAFE.

Out of the night, Villanazul strolls as nonchalantly as possible. Angled across stage right is the front of the café
with swinging doors and a great flake-painted glass window through which one can peer through those places
where the paint has snowed away.

Villanazul pretends not to be interested in the café or anything inside it, but at least he is drawn to peer in the
door at the darkness from which voices murmur. He then
puts his eye to a flaked place on the window and stands
thus until:

Manulo enters, looking back, wondering if he is being followed. He ducks into a setback near the café and peers
out, at which point Dominguez comes mysteriously on.
Manulo snorts and steps out.

MANULO

Caramba, it's you!

DOMINGUEZ

Manulo! What you doing here?

MANULO

(*lying badly*)
I was looking for a good place
to have a drink.

DOMINGUEZ

I was just walking, myself.
There's a good place.
(*points*)

MANULO

(*amazed*)
Sure! The Red Rooster Café.
Why didn't *I* think of that!

DOMINGUEZ

So many places, they're crowded.
Let's look before we go.

They line up with Villanazul, one on each side, peering
through the flaked glass. Once they are half-bent, Villanazul becomes sentient, he feels them on the other side, but
does not look yet.

MANULO

What do you see?

DOMINGUEZ

Nothing.

VILLANAZUL

He's in there, OK.

MANULO

(*looks up*)
Who is?

DOMINGUEZ

(*the same*)
Where!

BOTH

(*turning*)
Villanazul!

VILLANAZUL

Manulo! Dominguez! What *you*
doing here?

BOTH

What! What?! Ha!

As if well rehearsed, all three turn back to the window
and search for the best peepholes. Now Gomez and Martinez hurry on, do a double take, and line up with them.
This time there are no greetings, no rationalizations.

GOMEZ

Is our white suit in there?

MARTINEZ

Wait! Sure! Way back in the dark
there!

MANULO

(*in awe*)
Hey, yeah . . . there's the suit, and, praise
God, Vamenos is still *in* it!

VILLANAZUL

It's moving! It's coming this way!

Off in the café we see a whiteness drifting.

MANULO

He's got money! He's going to
play the jukebox!

The whiteness moves. We hear a fearful clangor of machinery as the money drops in and is digested. There is a vast hiss. Then, in one blast of light and sound, a huge behemoth of a jukebox explodes into color and brilliance, at the same time emitting such concussive brass and tympani that the five men are jarred from the window. Now, in full rainbow light, we see the suit, and Vamenos. He stands delightfully drenched with music, like a child out in the welcome rains of summer.

Vamenos lifts his hand. A glass is in it.

MANULO

He's drinking!

The men gasp. Inside, Vamenos sips wine.

VILLANAZUL

He's smoking.

Inside, Vamenos scatters sparks, blows smoke.

MARTINEZ

He's—eating!

It isn't easy, but juggling the items around in his hands, Vamenos shifts his cigar, his glass, and raises food to his mouth.

DOMINGUEZ

A taco!

GOMEZ

(*turns away*)
No!

MANULO

A *juicy* taco!

That's what it is. A very juicy taco that Vamenos has to
lean in at, arching his body so it won't drop on the clothes.

> VILLANAZUL
> *Ay, caramba!*

> GOMEZ
> What's he doing now?

> MARTINEZ
> Dancing!

> GOMEZ
> Dancing!!???

> VILLANAZUL
> With the cigar, the wine, and
> the taco!

> MANULO
> (*moving his feet and hips*)
> The Enchilada Cha-Cha-Cha. That's
> a good tune.

> GOMEZ
> (*enraged*)
> Good *tune?* It's our funeral march!

> MARTINEZ
> Hold everything! Someone's coming
> to dance with him!

> GOMEZ
> (*eyes closed*)
> Wait! Don't tell me! The big one ...
> weighs two hundred pounds on the
> hoof? Ruby Escuadrillo?

A woman who is as big, colorful and impressive as the
jukebox dances out of the shadows and circles Vamenos.

ALL

(*gasping*)
Ruby Escuadrillo!

Gomez must turn back now and look in.

GOMEZ

That ox! That hippo!

MARTINEZ

She's crushing the shoulder pads!

It's true. She has hold of one of the shoulders of the white
suit with her huge hand.

DOMINGUEZ

They've stopped dancing.

MARTINEZ

They're going to sit down. She's
going to sit in his lap!

VILLANAZUL

No, not with all that powder and
lipstick!

GOMEZ

Manulo! Inside! Grab that drink!
Villanazul, the cigar! Dominguez,
the taco! Martinez, dance Ruby
Escuadrillo away!

ALL

Aye! Check! Right! Done!

They start to move, but freeze when:

A great two-ton truck of a man lumbers into sight from
the street beyond, and pushes them out of the way, going
into the café.

MARTINEZ

Toro!

VILLANAZUL

Hi, Toro!

GOMEZ

Toro? Was that Toro Ruiz? Ruby
Escuadrillo's boyfriend?

MANULO

Sure!

MARTINEZ

If he finds her with Vamenos!

MANULO

The white suit!

VILLANAZUL

It'll be covered with blood!

GOMEZ

Don't make me nervous! Quick!
As before; taco, drink, cigar,
Ruby. Me! I'm for Toro Ruiz!

MANULO

What a brave one, you, Gomez!

GOMEZ

Andale!

They all rush in and collide to a halt for they see:

Toro Ruiz, who has discovered Vamenos and Ruby, just
as Ruby, laughing, sits down on Vamenos's lap.

Bellowing, Toro runs forward. Ruby jumps up.

GOMEZ

Wait!

Toro, his hand out, freezes. Villanazul runs, grabs the cigar out of Vamenos's mouth, smokes it. From here on, everyone moves in slow motion. They also speak in slow motion.

                    VILLANAZUL
          (*puffs*)
     I need a smoke!

                    VAMENOS
          (*surprised*)
     Hey!

Manulo grabs the glass, slowly.

                    MANULO
          (*gulps*)
     I need a drink!

                    VAMENOS
          (*upset*)
     Hey!

Dominguez seizes the taco, in slow motion.

                    DOMINGUEZ
          (*chewing*)
     I'm hungry!

                    VAMENOS
          (*irritated*)
     Hey!

Martinez grabs Ruby, slowly.

                    MARTINEZ
     Ruby! Ruby!

He dances her off, slowly.

                    VAMENOS and TORO
          (*angrily*)
     Hey!

Vamenos jumps up. Toro thinks he is being attacked and
catches Vamenos. He grabs several yards of lapel and
squashes it, but all with beautiful slow motion precision.

TORO

You! You!

At which all six owners of the suit yell, slowly.

GOMEZ

Let go!

MARTINEZ

Let go of Vamenos!

VILLANAZUL

No, let go the *suit!*

TORO

You dance, hah?

VAMENOS

No!

TORO

You tired, hah? I help you!

He dangles Vamenos like a marionette, so Vamenos tap-
dances in spite of himself. Toro cocks a fist, slowly.

Gomez thinks quickly and steps in, slowly.

GOMEZ

(*smiles*)
Don't hit *him*. Hit *me*.

Toro hits him smack on the nose.

Gomez holds his nose and wanders off, tears stinging his
eyes.

GOMEZ

Chi-hua-hua . . .

Villanazul grabs one of Toro's arms, Manulo the other.

MANULO
You're wrinkling the lapels!

VILLANAZUL
You're ripping the buttons!

VAMENOS
You're killing *me!*

DOMINGUEZ
Peon! Drop him! Let go!

MANULO
Cabron! Coyote! Vaca!

Toro wrenches the suit. All the men twist, wrench, in pantomime, with the agonized torture of the suit.

VILLANAZUL
Vamenos, go with the motion!
Don't fight. Where the suit goes,
go! Otherwise—

Toro cocks his fist again, and in doing so, shakes Manulo free, as easily as knocking a poker chip from his elbow.

TORO
Now!

Gomez wanders back, just in time.

GOMEZ
(*smiling bravely, holding his nose*)
Don't hit him. Hit *me.*

Toro beams. Toro hits Gomez on both the nose and the hand holding the nose. Gomez puts the damaged hand under his other arm and puts a new hand up to his freshly mangled nose, wandering off.

GOMEZ

Chee-wah-wah . . .

At which point a chair, beautifully uplifted by Martinez, comes down on Toro's head.

ALL

Aiiieeeeee!

They all stand back, waiting.

Toro shakes his head and carefully thinks over the facts: he has been hit; maybe, maybe he will not fall down. He cannot quite make up his mind. He sways. The men sway. He turns, dragging Vamenos, by the suit, with him. The men turn.

Now, slowly, Toro starts to sink down, down. But he still has hold of the lapels.

The men shout in at him, as if he were a long way off, and needs urgent instruction.

MANULO

Toro!

VILLANAZUL

The suit! The lapels!

GOMEZ

Let *go!*

Toro seems to hear their faint far calling. His glazed eyes flicker. But still he sinks.

ALL

Let . . . go!

And at the last moment, Toro blessedly opens his huge banana fingers.

Vamenos falls into the arms of his *compadres*.

Toro, like a poled ox, topples over, kicks, and lies, smiling foolishly. Instantly, the slow motion stops. From here on, everything returns to normal motion.

VAMENOS

(blinks)
Hey . . . what's going on?

GOMEZ

What?! *Compadres!* Out!

Vamenos is helped, lifted, carried around the ruin.

VAMENOS

Wait a minute! My drink! My
taco! Ruby!

The doors slam shut. As they do so, the lights flash off. The jukebox goes off. The interior of the café vanishes from view, Ruby and Toro with it.

Outside, the men hold Vamenos.

VAMENOS

Put me down!

Gomez nods. They put him down. The picture of outraged dignity, Vamenos brushes the suit, fixes his tie, shakes away their hands which try to adjust the lapels and button the buttons.

VAMENOS

OK, OK. My time ain't up!

ALL

(incredulous at his temerity)
What!

Vamenos takes Gomez's wrist to peer at the watch.

VAMENOS

I still got two minutes and—let's
see—ten seconds—

GOMEZ

Ten sec—you! You dance with a
Guadalajara cow! You smoke, you
drink, you eat tacos, you pick
fights, and now you got the nerve
to say you got two minutes and
ten seconds—

VAMENOS
(*nervously*)
Two minutes flat, now!

A woman's voice from off, away somewhere.

THE VOICE

Hey, Vamenos!

VAMENOS

Who's that?

THE VOICE
(*calling*)
Vamenos! Here! Ramona!

VAMENOS

It's Ramona. Hey, Ramona!

THE VOICE
Vamenos, you sure look sharp!

All the men have turned to look off across the street.

VAMENOS
Ramona, wait! I'm coming over!

GOMEZ
Vamenos, come back! The street!

MANULO

What can you do in one minute and—
(*checks watch*)
—forty seconds?

VAMENOS

(*winks*)
Watch! Ramona, here I come!

He runs off into darkness.

GOMEZ

Vamenos! Watch out!

MARTINEZ

That car!

MANULO

Jump!

We hear the car, the brakes, the horn. Out of sight, we hear Vamenos cry out.

ALL

Aaiiieeee . . . no!

A light flashes across the stage. The men all hold onto each other in fright, looking off, gabbling, no, no. Their heads move up over and along.

Vamenos is hurled backward out of darkness, falls on his back, rolls over and lies on his face, still.

The car guns its motor and races off. Gomez looks at the silent figure of Vamenos. Then suddenly it hits him what has happened and he runs a few steps after the car.

GOMEZ

Fiends! Fools! Murderers!
Come back, come back!
(*he stops and sways*)

Kill me, someone. I don't want
to live.

But the car is gone.

Now all the men stand breathing hard, unable to move.
They hold to each other a moment longer. Then the smallest
motion from Vamenos sets them walking, shambling, then
running to surround him. They stand looking down.

GOMEZ

Vamenos! You're . . . alive!

Vamenos has his eyes shut, his hands clenched at his sides,
his whole body stiff. He moans, he cries out.

VAMENOS

Tell me, tell me, oh, tell me,
tell me.

MANULO

Tell you what, Vamenos?

VAMENOS

Tell me . . .

He stops to grind his teeth, to moan.

The men crouch lower.

VAMENOS

What have I done . . . to the suit,
the suit, oh, the suit . . . ?

The men touch him.

VILLANAZUL

Vamenos . . . why . . .

MARTINEZ

It's OK . . . !

VAMENOS

(*eyes still shut*)
You lie! It's torn, it must be,
and around, underneath . . . ?

They touch him further, they handle him gently, they turn
him over.

GOMEZ

No. Vamenos, all around, underneath, on top, it's OK!

VAMENOS

(*opens his eyes*)
A miracle! Praise the saints!
Oh, good, good!

Distantly a siren wails. The men look up.

DOMINGUEZ

Someone must've phoned for an
ambulance!

VAMENOS

(*stricken*)
An ambulance! Quick! Set me up!
Take off our coat!

MANULO

Vamenos, you—

GOMEZ

Don't worry, we—

VAMENOS

(*rolling his eyes, gibbering*)
Idiots! The coat! The coat! Get it
off me!

They humor him, lift him, start to take it off. The siren is
louder.

VAMENOS
Yes, yes, that's it! Quick! There!

They have the coat off.

VAMENOS
Now, *andale,* the pants!

ALL
The pants?!

VAMENOS
The pants, the pants, fools! Lost
ones! Quick, *peones!* Those doctors!

GOMEZ
Doctors?

VAMENOS
You seen the movies!

MARTINEZ
Movies?

VAMENOS
In the movies they rip the pants
with razors to get them off! They
don't care! They're maniacs!

ALL
Maniacs!

They fly to work. Zip, zip, the pants are coming off now in
a frenzy.

VAMENOS
Ah, God, careful! Ah, ah! Jesus,
come after me, there, quick! The
siren!

GOMEZ
Here it comes! The ambulance!

Everyone handles Vamenos at once.

VAMENOS

Right leg, easy, hurry, cows! Left
leg, now, left, Ow, God . . . Martinez,
now, your pants!

MARTINEZ

Mine?

VAMENOS

Take them off!

MARTINEZ

What?

ALL

Off! Fool! All is lost!

Gomez flips at Martinez's belt buckle swiftly. Martinez falls
to and, hopping about, starts to get his pants off.

VAMENOS

Give me! Give!

GOMEZ

Form a circle! In! In!
Close in!

The men circle Martinez. We see his pants flourished on the
air. We see the white pants fly upward on the air.

VAMENOS

Quick, here come the maniacs with
the razors. Right leg, right!
Yes! Ah! Left leg, easy, ah-ow!

The men bend, leaving Martinez to hop around getting into
the white pants. The siren pulls up offstage and dies. A
light from the ambulance has flushed the stage.

VAMENOS
The zipper, cows! Zip my zipper! Ow!

The ambulance men run onstage with a portable carrier.
Vamenos lies back down, exhaling.

VAMENOS
Madre mia, just in time. *Gracias,*
compadres, gracias.

Martinez strolls off away, casually buckling the belt on the
white trousers. The ambulance men bend and examine
Vamenos.

ONE INTERN
Broken leg. What happened?

GOMEZ
He—

VAMENOS
(*quickly*)
I fell down . . . running after a
woman.

The interns look from Vamenos to the others, expectantly.
At last, Gomez nods.

GOMEZ
(*quietly*)
He fell down . . . running after a
woman.

They are all proud of Vamenos and his fine lie, in this moment. Now he is placed on the canvas carrier gently by the
men. Martinez has put on the white coat.

VAMENOS
Compadres . . . ? Don't be mad with me.

VILLANAZUL
Who's mad?

Now the carrier is lifted and the men stand around Vamenos as he speaks, faltering.

> VAMENOS
>
> *Compadres,* when . . . when I come from
> the hospital . . . am I still in the
> bunch?

There is a long silence.

> VAMENOS
>
> You won't kick me out? Look,
> I'll give up smoking, keep away
> from Murillo's, swear off women—

> MARTINEZ
>
> (*gently*)
> Vamenos. Don't promise nothing.

Vamenos looks at Martinez, his eyes brimming.

> VAMENOS
>
> Oh, Martinez, you sure look great
> in our suit. *Compadres,* don't he
> look beautiful?

They carry Vamenos out.

> VILLANAZUL
>
> Vamenos, I'll go with you!

Villanazul waves to the others and hurries out.

> MANULO
>
> I'll go with you, Vamenos!

> GOMEZ
>
> Me, we'll *all* go with you, Vamenos!

The siren brays. The guitar music plays. The men run out. Darkness.

When the light comes on again it is the raw overhead bulb

in the tenement room under which stands Dominguez iron-
ing the white coat on a board. Martinez stands nearby with
the pants over his arm. Now Dominguez finishes and holds
up the coat.

DOMINGUEZ
There! Clean, pressed! White as
a gardenia! Sharp as a razor!

They place the suit on the dummy and stand back.

GOMEZ
So . . . it's late. Two o'clock.
Friends, the room is yours.
Sleep.

He nods, he waves about. The men move to collapsible
cots. Some lie on the floor. But they make a circle, en-
closing the suit on the dummy. They all lie, looking at its
whiteness. Martinez alone remains standing by the suit,
fixing its lapels.

MARTINEZ
Ay, caramba, what a night. Seems
ten years since seven o'clock, when
it all started and I had no friends.
Two in the morning I got all *kinds*
of friends. Even Celia Obregon, the
girl in the window. All kinds of
friends. I got a room. I got
clothes. You tell *me*. Hey!
    (*softly*)
Funny. When I wear this suit, I know
I will win at pool like Gomez. I
will sing and play the guitar like
Manulo. I will dance like Dominguez.
I will talk fine talk like Villanazul.
Be strong in the arms like Vamenos . . .

So . . . so, tonight I am Gomez, Manulo,
Dominguez, Villanazul, Vamenos.
Everyone . . . *Ay . . . ay . . .*

There is a moment of silence. Outside, flushing in through
the windows, we see the light of various neon signs flashing
on and off. Martinez stands musing.

GOMEZ

(*quietly*)
Martinez? You going to sleep?

MARTINEZ

Sure. I'm just—thinking.

MANULO

What?

MARTINEZ

(*softly*)
If we ever get rich, it'll be kind
of sad. Then we'll all have suits.
And there won't be no more nights
like tonight. It'll break up the
old gang. It'll never be the same after that.

The men lie thinking of it for a moment.

Gomez nods at last, a sudden sadness in his voice.

GOMEZ

Yeah . . . it'll never be the same . . .
after that.

Martinez pulls the light cord. The light goes out. From
outside the neon lights flash on and off, on and off.

Martinez strokes the white suit a last time, then lies down
near it.

The men look at the suit in the flashing on-and-off light.

It stands in the middle of the room, in the middle of their lives, white in darkness, now seen, now vanishing, now seen, now vanishing, as the neon lights flash, flash, and again flash, flash, and the guitar plays slow, slow, a chord, another sweet, sad chord and

the curtain slowly, slowly descends.

THE END

The Veldt

The curtain rises to find a completely empty room with no furniture of any kind in it. This room encompasses the entire front half of the stage. Its walls are scrim which appear when lighted from the front, vanish when lighted from the rear. In the center of the room is a door which leads to the living quarters of a house circa 1991. The living quarters dominate the entire rear half of the stage. There we see armchairs, lamps, a dining table and chairs, some abstract paintings. When the characters in the play are moving about the living area, the lights in the "empty" room, the playroom, will be out, and we will be able to see through into the back quarters of the house. Similarly, when the characters enter the empty playroom, the lights will vanish in the living room and come on, in varying degrees, as commanded, in the play area.

At rise of curtain, the playroom is dimly lit. An electrician, bent to the floor, is working by flashlight, fingering and testing electrical equipment set under a trapdoor. From above and all around come ultrahigh-frequency hummings and squealings, as volume and tone are adjusted.

George Hadley, about thirty-six, enters and moves through the living area to look through the playroom door. He is fascinated, delighted in fact, by the sounds and the flicker of shadows in the playroom. He looks out through the fourth wall, as he will do often in the play, and treats the audience area, on all sides, as if it were the larger part of the playroom. Much lighting, and vast quantities of sound, will come from the sides and back of the theater itself.

At last, excited, George turns and calls.

GEORGE

Lydia! Lydia, come here!

She appears, a woman about thirty-two, very clean and fresh, dressed simply but expensively for a housewife.

> GEORGE
> (*waving*)
> Come on! It's almost ready!

She joins him at the door as the humming, squealing dies. The electrician slams the trapdoor, rises, and comes toward them with his kit.

> THE ELECTRICIAN
> It's all yours, Mr. Hadley.

> GEORGE
> Thanks, Tom.

The electrician turns to point a screwdriver into the room.

> ELECTRICIAN
> There's your new—how does
> the advertisement read?—
> Happylife Electrodynamic
> Playroom! And *what* a room!

> LYDIA
> (*ruefully*)
> It ought to be. It cost
> thirty thousand dollars.

> GEORGE
> (*taking her arm*)
> You'll forget the cost when you
> see what the room can do.

> ELECTRICIAN
> You sure you know how to work it?

> GEORGE
> You taught me well!

ELECTRICIAN

I'll run on, then. Wear it
in health!
  (*exits*)

GEORGE

Good-bye, Tom.

George turns to find Lydia staring into the room.

GEORGE

Well!

LYDIA

Well ...

GEORGE

Let me call the children!

He steps back to call down a hall.

GEORGE

Peter! Wendy!
  (*winks at his wife*)
They wouldn't want to miss this.

The boy and the girl, twelve and thirteen, respectively, appear after a moment. Both are rather pale and look as if they slept poorly. Peter is engrossed in putting a point to his sister as they enter.

PETER

Sure, I know, I know, you
don't like fish. OK.
But fish is one thing and
fishing is something else!
  (*turning*)
Dad and I'll catch whoppers,
won't we, dad?

                                   GEORGE
             (*blinking*)
             What, what?

                                   PETER
             (*apprehensively*)
             Fishing. Loon Lake. You
             remember . . . *today* . . .
             you promised . . .

                                   GEORGE
             Of course. Yes.

A buzzer and bell cut in. A TV screen, built into one wall
at an angle so we cannot see it, flashes on and off. George
jabs a button. We see the flickering shadows on his face as
the screen glows.

                                   GEORGE
             Yes?

                         SECRETARY'S RADIO VOICE
             Mr. Hadley . . .

                                   GEORGE
             (*aware of his son's eyes*)
             Yes? yes . . .

                         SECRETARY'S VOICE
             A special board meeting is
             called for 11. A helicopter
             is on its way to pick you up.

                                   GEORGE
             I . . . thanks.

George snaps the screen off, but cannot turn to face his
son.

GEORGE

I'm sorry, Peter. They own
me, don't they?

Peter nods mutely.

LYDIA

(*helpfully*)
Well, now, it isn't all bad.
Here's the new playroom
finished and ready.

GEORGE

(*hearing*)
Sure, sure ... you children don't
know how lucky you are.

The children stare silently into the room, as George opens
the door very wide so we get a good view.

WENDY

Is that all there is to it?

PETER

But—it's *empty*.

GEORGE

It only *looks* empty. It's
a machine, but more than a
machine!

He has fallen into the salesman's cadence as he tries to
lead the children through the door. They will not move.
Perturbed, he reaches in past them and touches a switch.
Immediately the room begins to hum. Slowly, George Hadley steps gingerly into the room.

GEORGE

Here, now. Watch me.
If you please.

George has addressed this last to the ceiling, in a pompous tone.

The humming becomes louder.

The children wait, unimpressed.

George glances at them and then says, quickly:

GEORGE
Let there be light.

The dull ceiling dissolves into very bright light as if the sun had come from a cloud! Electronic music begins to build edifices of sound.

The children, startled, shield their eyes, looking in at their father.

GEORGE
Paris. The blue hour of twilight.
The gold hour of sunset. An
Eiffel Tower, please, of bronze!
An Arc de Triomphe of shining
brass! Let fountains toss forth
fiery lava. Let the Seine be a
torrent of gold!

The light becomes golden within the room, bathing him.

GEORGE
Egypt now! Shape pyramids of
white-hot stone. Carve Sphinx
from ancient sand! There! There!
Do you see, children? Come in!
Don't stand out there!

The children, standing on either side of the door, do not move. George pretends not to notice.

GEORGE
Enough! Begone!

The lights go out, leaving only a dim light spotted on George's face. The electronic music dies.

GEORGE
There! What do you think, eh?

WENDY
It's great.

GEORGE
Great? It's a miracle, that's
what it is. There's a giant's eye,
a giant's ear, a giant's brain in
each of those walls, that remembers
every city, town, hill, mountain,
ocean, every birdsong, every language,
all the music of the world. In three
dimensions, by God. Name anything.
The room will hear and obey.

PETER
(*looking steadily at him*)
You sound like a salesman.

GEORGE
(*off balance*)
Do I? Well, no harm. We all have
some melodrama in us needs bleeding
out on occasion. Tones the system
Go in, kids, go on.

Wendy creeps in a toe. Peter does not move.

GEORGE
Peter, you heard me!

Helicopter thunder floods the house. All look up. Huge shadows flutter in a side window. George, relieved, breaks, moves from the room.

GEORGE

There's my helicopter. Lydia,
will you see me to the door?

LYDIA

(*hesitating*)
George . . . ?

GEORGE

(*still moving*)
Have fun, kids!
(*stops, suddenly, thinking*)
Peter? Wendy? Not even "Thanks"?

WENDY

(*calmly*)
Thanks a lot, dad.

She nudges Peter, who does not even look at his father.

PETER

(*quietly*)
Thanks . . .

The children, left behind, turn slowly to face the door of
the playroom. Wendy puts one hand into the room. The
room hums, strangely, now, at her approach. It is a different
sound from the one we heard when George entered the
place. The hum now has an *atonal* quality.

Wendy moves out into the empty space, turns, and waits
for Peter to follow, reluctantly. The humming grows.

WENDY

I don't know what to ask it for.
You. Go ahead. Please. Ask it
to show us something.

Peter relents, shuts his eyes, thinks, then whispers.

WENDY

What? I didn't hear you.

PETER

The room did. Look.

He nods. Shadows stir on the walls, colors dilate. The children look about, obviously fascinated at what is only suggested to the audience.

WENDY

That's a lake. *Loon* Lake!

PETER

Yes.

WENDY

Oh, it's so blue! It's like the
sky turned upside down. And there's
a boat, white as snow, on the water!
It's moving toward us.

We hear the sound of water lapping, the sound of oars at a distance.

WENDY

Someone's rowing the boat.

PETER

A boy.

WENDY

Someone's behind the boy.

PETER

A man.

WENDY

Why, it's you, and dad!

PETER

Is it? Yes. Now we've stopped, the
lines are out, fishing.
(*suddenly excited*)
There. I've caught a big one!
A big one!

We hear a distant splash of water.

WENDY

It's beautiful. It's all silver coins!

PETER

It's a beaut, all right. Boy! Boy!

WENDY

Oh, it slipped off the line! It's
gone!

PETER

That isn't—

WENDY

(*disappointed*)
The boat . . . it's going away. The
fog's coming up. I can hardly see
the boat . . . or you or dad.

PETER

Neither can I . . .

WENDY

(*forlorn*)
The boat's gone. Bring it back,
Peter.

PETER

Come back!

An echo, way off, repeats his words. The playroom grows
dimmer.

PETER

It's no use. The room's broken.

WENDY

You're not trying. Come back!
Come back!

PETER

Come back!

Lydia enters on this last, slightly concerned.

LYDIA

Peter, Wendy? Is everything
all right?

PETER

Sure, swell . . .

LYDIA

(*checks her watch*)
Have you tried Mexico yet? The
instructions book said the most
wonderful things about the Aztec
ruins there. Well! I'll be downtown at 10:45, at Mrs. Morgan's at
11:30, at Mrs. Harrison's at noon,
if you should want me. The
automatic lunch timer will go off
at 12:15, eat, both of you! At
one o'clock do your musical tapes
with the violin and piano. I've
written the schedule on the electric
board—

PETER

Sure, mom, sure—

LYDIA

Have fun, and don't forget Bombay,
India, while you're at it!

She exits and is hardly gone when: a thunderous roar ensues. Peter, throwing out one hand, pointing at the walls, has given a shout.

PETER

All right! Now! Now! Now!

An unseen avalanche thunders down a vast mountain in torrents of destruction. Wendy seizes Peter's arm.

WENDY

Peter!

PETER

Now! More! More!

WENDY

Peter, stop it!

The avalanche filters away to dust and silence.

WENDY

What are you doing? What was that?

PETER
(*looks at her strangely*)
Why, an avalanche, of course. I
made an avalanche come down a
mountain, a hundred thousand tons
of stone and rocks. An avalanche.

WENDY
(*looking about*)
You filled the lake. It's gone. The
boat's gone. You and dad are gone.

PETER

Did I? Is it? Are they?

PETER

   (*awed*)
Yeah . . . sure . . . that's right.
Hey, this is . . . *fun* . . .
   (*he accents this last word oddly*)
You try something now, Wendy.

WENDY

I—London Bridge. Let me see—
London Bridge.

The shadows spin slowly. Peter and Wendy stand, watching.

PETER

You're stupid. That's no fun.
Think, girl, think! Now! Let's see.
   (*a beat*)
Let there be darkness!
Let there be—night!

Blackout.

The lights come up. We hear a helicopter come down, fly away. George enters, stage left.

GEORGE

Hi! I'm home!

In a small alcove, which represents only a section of the kitchen, far stage right, Lydia is seated staring at a machine that is mixing something for her.

George advances across the stage.

GEORGE

Hi! How goes it?

LYDIA

(*looking up*)
Oh, hello. Fine.

GEORGE

Perfect, you mean. Flying home
just now I thought, Good Lord,
what a house! We've lived in it
since the kids were born, never
lacked for a thing. A great life.
Incredible.

LYDIA

It's incredible, all right, but—

GEORGE

But what?

LYDIA

This kitchen. I don't know.
It's—*selfish*. Sometimes I think
it'd be happy if I just stayed out,
stayed away completely, and let it
work.
   (*she tries to smile*)
Aren't I silly?

GEORGE

You are indeed. All these time-
saving devices; no one on the block
has half as many.

LYDIA

   (*unconvinced*)
You're right, of course.
   (*she pauses*)
George . . . I want you to look at
the playroom.

GEORGE

Look at it? Is it broken? Good
Lord, we've only had it eight weeks.

LYDIA

No, not broken, exactly. Well,
see it first, then you tell *me*.

She starts leading him across the stage.

GEORGE

Fair enough. Lead on, Macduff.

LYDIA

I first noticed this "thing" I'm
going to show you about four weeks
ago. Then it kept reoccurring.
I didn't want to worry you, but now,
with the thing happening all the
time—well—*here*.

She opens the playroom door. George steps in and looks
as across a great distance, silently.

GEORGE

Lord, but it's quiet.

LYDIA

Too quiet, yes.

GEORGE

Don't tell me. I know right off.
This is—Africa.

LYDIA

Africa.

GEORGE

Good Lord, is there a child in the
world hasn't wanted to go to Africa?

Is there one exists who can't close
his eyes and paint the whole thing
on his inner lids? High blue deep
warm sky. Horizons a billion miles
off in the dust that smells like
pulverized honeybees and old manu-
scripts and cloves and cinnamons.
Boma-trees, veldtland. And a lush
smell. Smell it?

LYDIA

Yes.

GEORGE

That must mean a water hole nearby, bwana.
   (*laughs*)
Oh, Lydia, it's perfect, perfect!
But—the sun—damn hot. Look,
a perfect necklace of sweat right
off the brow!
   (*shows her*)
But I've lost the point. You
brought me here because you were
worried. Well—I see nothing to
worry about.

LYDIA

Wait a moment. Let it sink in.

GEORGE

Let *what* sink in? I—

Shadows flick over their faces. He looks quizzically up.
She does, too, with distaste. We hear a dry rustling leathery
sound from above; distant strange bird cries.

LYDIA

Filthy things.

GEORGE
(*looking up, following
the circling birds*)
What? Vultures? Yes, God made
his ugliest kites on the day he
sent those things sailing. Is
that what worries you?

LYDIA
That's only part of it. Look around.

George turns slowly. There is a heavy, rich purring rumble
from off to the right. George blinks and smiles.

GEORGE
It couldn't be—the lions?

LYDIA
I think so, yes. I don't like—
having lions in the house.

GEORGE
(*amused*)
Well, they're not exactly *in* the
house, dear. There! Look at that
big male. Face like a blast furnace
at high noon, and a mane like a field
of wheat. Burns your eyes to look
at him. There's another—a female—
and another, a whole pride—
isn't that a fine word? A pride—
a regular tapestry of lions woven
of gold thread and sunlight.
(*an afterthought*)
What are they up to?

He turns to Lydia, who is watching the unseen beasts, disquieted.

LYDIA

I think they're—feeding.

GEORGE

On what?
     (*squints*)
Zebra or
baby giraffe, I imagine.

LYDIA

Are you certain?

GEORGE

     (*shielding his eyes*)
Well, it's a bit late to be certain
of anything. They've been lunching
quite some time. No—lunch is
over. There they go toward the
water hole!
     (*he follows with his eyes*)

LYDIA

George? On our way down the hall
just now . . . did you . . . hear a
scream from in here?

GEORGE

     (*glances at her*)
A scream? No. For God's sake—

LYDIA

All right. Forget it. It's just,
the lions won't go away.

GEORGE

What do you mean? Won't go?

LYDIA

Nor will Africa, either. George,
the fact is, the room has stayed

that way for 31 days. Every day
that same yellow sun in the sky.
Every day the lions with teeth like
daggers dusting their pelts out
there, killing, slavering on the
red-hot meat, printing their bloody
tracks through the trees, killing,
gorging, over and over, no day
different, no hour any change.
Doesn't it strike you as odd that
the children never ask for a
different locale?

GEORGE
No! They must love Africa as all
kids do. The smell of violence.
Life stark, raw, visceral. Here,
you, hey! Hey!

He snaps his fingers, points, snaps his fingers again. He
turns smiling to Lydia.

GEORGE
You see, they come to pay their respects.

LYDIA
(*nervously; gasps*)
Oh, George, not so close!

The rumbling of the lions is very loud now, to the right,
we feel the approach of the beasts. The light from the
right side of the room becomes more brightly yellow.

GEORGE
Lydia, you're not afraid?

LYDIA
No, no, it's just—don't you
feel it? It's almost as if they
can see us!

GEORGE

Yes, the illusion *is* three-
dimensional. Pure fire, isn't
he? There. There.
   (*holds out his hands*)
You can warm yourself at a hearth
like that. Listen to him breathe,
it's like a beehive swarming with
yellow.

He stretches one hand further out.

GEORGE

You feel you could just—reach—
and run your hand over the bronze,
the gold—

LYDIA

   (*screams*)
Look out!

There is a fearful snarling roar. The shadows race in the
room. Lydia falls back, runs, George, startled, cannot stop
her, so follows. She slams the door and falls against it.
He is laughing. She is almost in tears.

GEORGE

Lydia, dear Lydia!

LYDIA

George, they almost—

GEORGE

Almost what? It's machinery,
electronics, sonics, visuals!

LYDIA

No, *more!* Much more! Now listen
to me, I insist, I insist, do you
hear, that you warn the children
this playing in Africa must cease!

GEORGE
(*comforting, kissing her*)
OK, I'll talk to them.

LYDIA
Talk to them, no; lay down the
law. Every day for a month I've
tried to get their attention.
But they just stroll off under
that damned hot African sky! Do
you remember that night three weeks
ago when you switched the whole
room off for 24 hours to punish
the children?

GEORGE
(*laughing quietly*)
Oh, how they hated me for that.
It's a great threat. If they
misbehave I'll shut it off again.

LYDIA
And they'll hate you again.

GEORGE
Let them. It's perfectly natural
to hate your father when he
punishes you.

LYDIA
Yes, but they don't say a word.
They just look at you. And day by
day, the playroom gets hotter, the
veldtland wider and more desolate,
and the lions grow big as the sun.

There is an awkward moment. Then a buzzer rings, loudly.
George presses a panel in the wall. A loudspeaker bell
sounds, there is a faint crackle and:

PETER'S VOICE
Mom, we won't be home for supper.

WENDY'S VOICE
We're at the automation show
across town, OK?

GEORGE
I think that—

PETER'S VOICE
Swell!

WENDY'S VOICE
Keen!

Buzz ding! Silence. Lydia stares at the ceiling from which
the voices came.

LYDIA
No hellos, no good-byes, no pleases,
no thank-yous.

George takes her hand.

GEORGE
Lydia, you've been working too hard.

LYDIA
Have I really? Then why is something
wrong with the room, and the house
and the four people who live in the
house?

She touches the playroom door.

LYDIA
Feel? It trembles as if a huge
bake oven were breathing against it.

She takes her hand off, burnt.

LYDIA

The lions—they can't come out,
can they? They can't?

George smiles, shakes his head. She hurries off.

GEORGE

Where are you going?

She pauses near the door.

LYDIA

Just to press the button . . . that
will make us our dinner.

She touches the wall panel. The lights go out.
End of scene.

In the dark, music. As the light comes up dimly again we find George in his easy chair, smoking his pipe, glancing at his watch, listening to the hi-fi system. After a moment, impatiently, he gets up and switches off the music. He moves next to the radio, switches it on, listens to a moment of news:

WEATHER VOICE

Weather in the city tomorrow
will be 66 in the morning,
70 in the afternoon, with
some chance of rain.

He cuts this off, too, checking his watch. Next he switches on a TV screen to one side, its face away from us. For a moment, the ghostly pallor of the screen fills the room. He winces, shuts it off. He lights his pipe. There is a bell sound.

LYDIA'S VOICE

George, are you in the living room?

GEORGE

I couldn't sleep.

LYDIA
The children *are* home, aren't they?

GEORGE

I waited up for them—
    (*finishes lamely*)
Not yet.

LYDIA
But it's midnight! I'll be down
in a minute—

GEORGE
Don't bother—

But the bell has rung. Lydia has cut off. George paces the
floor, taps out his pipe, starts to reload it, looks at the playroom door, decides against it, looks again, and finally approaches it. He turns the knob and lets it drift open.

Inside the room it is darker. George is surprised.

GEORGE
Hello, what? Is the veldt gone?
Wait—no. The sun's gone down.
The vultures have flown into the
trees far over there. Twilight.
Bird cries. Stars coming out.
There's the crescent moon. But
where—? So you're *still* there, are you?

There is a faint purring.

GEORGE
What are you waiting for, eh?
Why don't you want to go away?

Paris, Cairo, Stockholm, London,
they and all their millions of
people swarmed out of this room
when told to leave. So why not you?
   (*snaps his fingers*)
Go!

The purring continues.

              GEORGE
A new scene, new place, new
animals, people! Let's have Ali
Baba and the Forty Thieves!
The Leaning Tower of Pisa! I
demand it, room! *Now!*

A jackal laughs off in the darkness.

              GEORGE
Shut up, shut up, shut up!
Change, change, now!
   (*his voice fades*)
. . . now . . .

The lions rumble. Monkeys gibber from distant trees. An elephant trumpets in the dusk. George backs off out the door. Slowly he shuts the door, as Lydia enters stage left.

              GEORGE
You're right . . . the fool room's
out of order. It won't obey.

              LYDIA
Won't, or *can't?*

She lights a candle on a table to one side.

GEORGE

Turn on the light. Why do you
fuss with candles like that?

She looks at the flame as she lights a second and a third
candle.

LYDIA

I rather like candles. There's
always the chance they will blow
out and then I can light them again.
Gives me something to do. Anything
else in the house goes wrong, electronic
doors don't slide or the garbage dis-
posal clogs, I'm helpless and must
call an engineer or a photoelectric
brain surgeon to put it right. So,
as I think I said, I like candles.

George has seated himself. Lydia turns to come to him now.

LYDIA

George, is it possible that since
the children have thought and
thought about Africa and lions
and those terrible vultures day after
day, the room has developed a
psychological "set"?

GEORGE

I'll call a repair man in the morning.

LYDIA

No. Call our psychiatrist.

George looks at her in amazement.

GEORGE

David Maclean?

LYDIA

(*steadily*)
Yes, David Maclean.

The front door springs open, Peter and Wendy run in laughing.

PETER

Last one there's an old maid
in a clock factory!

WENDY

Not me, not me!

GEORGE

Children!

The children freeze.

GEORGE

Do you know what time it is?

PETER

Why, it's midnight, of course.

GEORGE

Of course? Are you in the habit
of coming in this late?

PETER

Sometimes, yes. Just last month,
remember, you had some friends
over, drinking, and we came in
and you didn't kick up a fuss, so—

GEORGE

Enough of that! We'll go into
this late-hour business again.
Right now I want to talk about
Africa! The playroom . . .

The children blink . . .

PETER

The playroom . . . ?

Lydia tries to do this lightly.

LYDIA

Your father and I were just
traveling through African veldtland;
lion grass, water holes, vultures,
all that.

PETER

I don't remember any Africa in
the playroom. Do you, Wendy?

WENDY

No . . .

They look at each other earnestly.

PETER

Run see and come tell.

Wendy bolts. George thrusts out his hand.

GEORGE

Wendy!

But she is gone through the door of the playroom. George
leaps up. Peter faces him calmly.

PETER

It's all right, George. She'll
look and give us a report.

GEORGE

I don't want a report. I've seen!
And stop calling me George!

PETER

(*serenely*)
All right—father.

GEORGE

Now get out of the way! Wendy!

Wendy runs back out.

WENDY

It's not Africa at *all!*

George stares, astonished at her nerve.

GEORGE

We'll see about that!

He thrusts the playroom door wide and steps through, startled.

Lush green garden colors surround him in the playroom. Robins, orioles, bluebirds sing in choirs, tree shadows blow on a bright wind over shimmering banks of flower colors.

Butterfly shadows tatter the air about George's face which, surprised, grows dark as he turns to:

The smiling children; they stop smiling.

GEORGE

You—

LYDIA

George!

GEORGE

She changed it from Africa to
this!

He jerks his hand at the tranquil, beautiful scene.

WENDY

Father, it's only Apple Valley
in April—

> GEORGE
> Don't lie to me! You changed
> it! Go to bed!

Peter takes Wendy's hand and backs out of the room. Their
parents watch them go, then turn to be surrounded again
by green leaf colors, butterfly shadows, and the singing of
the birds.

> LYDIA
> George, are you sure you didn't
> change the scene yourself,
> accidentally?

> GEORGE
> It wouldn't change for me or
> you. The children have spent
> so much time here, it only obeys
> them.

> LYDIA
> Oh, God, I'm sorry, sorry, sorry
> you had this room built!

He gazes around at the green shadows, the lovely flecks of
spring light.

> GEORGE
> No. No, I see now, that in the
> long run, it may help us in a
> roundabout way, to see our children
> clearly. I'll call our psychiatrist
> first thing tomorrow.

> LYDIA
> (relieved)
> Good, Oh good . . .

They start to move from the room. Lydia stops and bends
to pick something from the floor.

LYDIA

Wait a moment.

GEORGE

What is it?

LYDIA

I don't know. What does it
look like, to you?

GEORGE
(*touches it*)
Leather. Why, it must be—
my old wallet!

LYDIA

What's happened to it?

GEORGE

Looks like it's been run through
a machine.

LYDIA

Or else—it's been chewed.
Look, all the teethmarks!

GEORGE

Teethmarks, hell! The marks of
cogs and wheels.

LYDIA

And this?

They turn the wallet between them.

GEORGE

The dark stuff? Chocolate, I
think.

LYDIA

Do you?

He sniffs the leather, touches it, sniffs again.

GEORGE

Blood.

The room is green spring around and behind them. The birds sing louder now, in the silence that follows the one word he has pronounced. George and Lydia look around at the innocent colors, at the simple and lovely view.

Far away, after a moment, we hear the faint trailing off of one scream, or perhaps two. We are not quite certain. George quickens.

LYDIA

There! You heard it! This
time, you *did!*

GEORGE

No.

LYDIA

You did. I know you did!

GEORGE

I heard nothing, nothing at all!
Good Lord, it's late, let's get
to bed!

He throws the wallet down, and hurries out.

After he is gone, Lydia picks up the shapeless wallet, turns it in her hands, and looks through the door of the play-room.

There the birds sing, the green-yellow shadows stir in leaf patterns everywhere, softly whispering. She describes it to herself.

LYDIA

. . . flowering apple tree . . .
peach blossoms . . . so white . . .

Behind her, in the living room, George blows out one candle.

LYDIA

... so lovely ...

He blows out the other candle. Darkness.

The scene is ended.

After a moment of silence and darkness, we hear a helicopter thunder down outside the house. A door opens. When it shuts, the lights come on, and George is leading David Maclean on.

GEORGE

Awfully nice of you to come
by so early, David.

DAVID

No bother, really, if you'll
give me my breakfast.

GEORGE

I'll fix it myself—or—
rather—almost fix it myself.
The room's there. I'm sure you'll
want to examine it alone, anyway.

DAVID

I would.

GEORGE

It's nothing, of course. In the
light of day, I see that. But—
go ahead. I'll be right back.

George exits. Maclean, who is carrying what looks like a medical kit, puts it down and takes out some tools. Small, delicate tools of the sort used to repair TV sets, unortho-

dox equipment for a psychiatrist. He opens a panel in the
wall. We see intricate film spools, lights, lenses there, re-
vealed for the first time. Maclean is checking it when the
playroom door opens and Peter comes out. The boy stops
when he sees Maclean.

> PETER
>
> Hello, who are you?

> DAVID
>
> David Maclean.

> PETER
>
> Electronics repair?

> DAVID
>
> Not exactly.

> PETER
>
> David Maclean. I know. You read
> the bumps on people's heads.

> DAVID
>
> I wish it were that simple. Right
> now I've come to see what you and
> your sister have written on the
> walls of this room.

> PETER
>
> We haven't written—oh, I see
> what you mean. Are you always this
> honest?

> DAVID
>
> People know when you lie.

> PETER
>
> But they don't! And you know why?
> They're not listening. They're
> turned to themselves. So you

might as well lie, since, in the
end, you're the only one awake.

DAVID

Do you really believe that?

PETER

(*truly amazed*)
I thought everyone did!

He grabs the playroom door as if to go back in.

DAVID

Please.

PETER

I must clean the room.

David steps between him and the door.

DAVID

If you don't mind, I'd *prefer*
it untidy.

Peter hesitates. They stare each other down.

PETER

All right. It doesn't matter.
Go ahead.

Peter walks off, circling once, then runs, gone.

Maclean looks after the boy, then turns to the door of the
playroom, and slowly opens it. From the color of the light
inside the room we can sense that it is Africa again. We
hear faint lion sounds, far off, and the distant leather
flapping of wings. Maclean looks around for only a moment, then kneels on the floor of the room where he
opens a trapdoor and looks down at intricate flickering machineries where firefly lights wink and glow and where
there is oiled secretive motion. He touches this button,
that switch, that bit of film, this sprocket, that dial.

In obedience to this, the light within the room gets fierce, oven-white, blinding as an atomic explosion, the screams get a bit louder, the roaring of the lions louder.

Maclean touches into the paneling again.

The roars get very loud, the screams very high and shrill, over and over, over and over as if repeated on a broken phonograph record. Maclean stands riven. There is a tremendous rustling of wings. The lion rumble fades. And as silence falls, the color of the walls of the room is stained by crimson flowing red until all is redness within the room, all is bleeding sunset light upon which, slowly, slowly, with grim thoughtfulness, David Maclean closes the trapdoor and backs out into the living room area.

Lydia enters with a tray on which is breakfast coffee and toast.

When she sees that Maclean is deep in thought, she says nothing, puts down the tray, pours coffee for three, at which point George enters and frowns when he sees Maclean's deep concern. The husband and wife look at each other, and wait. Maclean at last comes over picks up his coffee, sips it thoughtfully, and at last speaks.

MACLEAN
George . . . Lydia . . .

He hesitates a moment, drinks more coffee, prepares himself.

MACLEAN
When I gave my approval of your
building that playroom it was
because the record in the past
with such playrooms has been

exceptionally good. They not
only provide imaginative
atmospheres wherein children
can implement their desires and
dreams, they also give us, if we
wish, as parents, teachers
psychiatrists, the opportunity
to study the patterns left on
the walls by the children's minds.
Road maps, as it were, which we
can look at in our leisure time
to see where our children are
going and how we can help them
on their way. We humans are
mostly inarticulate, there is so
much we wish to say we cannot say,
so the rooms, and the walls of
such rooms, offered a way of
speaking out with the silent
tongue of the mind. In 99 cases
out of 100, it works. Children
use the rooms, parents observe
the blueprints marked on the walls
of the rooms, and everyone is
happy. But in this case—
  (*he stops*)

LYDIA

This case?

MACLEAN

I'm afraid the room has become
a channel *toward* destructive
thoughts rather than a release
away from them. George . . .

Lydia . . . why do your children
hate you so much?

LYDIA
(*surprised*)
Hate us? They don't hate us!

GEORGE
We're their parents!

MACLEAN
Are you really? Let's see.

Maclean paces the room, pointing out this door, indicating
that machine panel, or another here or there.

MACLEAN
What kind of life do you lead?
Machines make your bed, shine
your shoes, blow your noses for
you. Machines listen for you,
learn for you, speak for you.
Machines ventilate your house,
drive you down the street at
ninety miles an hour, or lift
you straight up into the sky,
Always away and away from your
home. I call on the phone and
another machine answers,
pre-recorded, and says you're
not here. How long has it been
since you got out of your car
and walked with your children
to find your *own* air, which means
air no one else has breathed,
outside of town? How long since
you flew a kite or picked do-it-
yourself wild strawberries? How
long? How long? How long?

Maclean sits. The parents are silent. Unnoticed, Peter and Wendy have come into the door at the far side of the room. Maclean drinks his coffee and finishes, as quietly as possible, thus:

MACLEAN

You haven't been around. And
since you haven't been around,
this house and its machines, that
playroom has become the only
available garden where your
children can take root. But when
you force-grow flowers in a
mechanical greenhouse, don't be
surprised if you wind up with
exotic orchids, strange tiger-
lilies or Venus's fly-traps.

GEORGE

What must we do?

MACLEAN

Now, very late, after playing an
idiot Father Christmas for years,
I'm going to ask you to play what
will seem like Ebenezer Scrooge
to your children.

George rises up and turns toward the playroom door.

GEORGE

You want me to switch off the
room?

MACLEAN

The room, the house, the damned
"sprinklers" in the lawn! Get out,
stay out, get away; send the kids
to me for treatment, but better

yet, treat them yourselves. Look
at them with your eyes, show them
your faces, talk to them not
on the intercom, but let them
feel your warm breath in their
ears, comb their hair with your
fingers, wash their backs with
your hands, sing to them, run
with them a little way before
they run so far ahead they run
out of your lives.

George moves toward the door.

GEORGE

But if I switch off the room,
the shock—

MACLEAN

Better a clean, hard shock now
than letting the kids get any
further from reality.

GEORGE

Yes . . . yes . . .

He opens the door of the room. Crimson light pours out.
The walls inside bleed with running color. Reacting to
this, George kneels to the panel in the floor and tears at it.

Suddenly, Peter stands out from the door.

PETER

George! No!

Maclean and Lydia are on their feet at this.

MACLEAN

Hold on, George.

Not with the children here.

George whips the panel open. Peter leaps forward and slams it shut.

PETER

No, George, no, no!

MACLEAN

Listen to me—wait!

GEORGE

Get out of the way.

PETER

George!

GEORGE

(*evenly*)
Don't call me George.

He thrusts the boy aside, gets the panel open, but the boy is scrabbling now. Screams well out the walls of the scarlet room in a tidal blast. Maclean and Lydia freeze as the boy and George fight over the switches. Heat shimmers, animal heartbeats ricochet from walls, avalanches of zebras panic away with okapi, gazelle, and wildebeest, thundering, shrieking.

George knocks Peter's hands off, twists and shoves him, and hits all the switches at once.

There are great elephant trumpetings, a final cry from many creatures now struck by electronic death, dying ... The sounds run down like a phonograph record. In a flush of red light, all the colors of the room dissolve like oil down the walls into the floor as blood might be let from a flask. Silence. The room shadows into darkness. George slams the trap and locks it with his key and stands on it. The only sound is Peter's sobbing and crying, slumped by George.

PETER

You! You!

GEORGE

(*to himself*)
Yes ... me ... me!

PETER

(*rising*)
You killed them! You killed
them! I hate you! I wish you
were dead! I wish you were
dead!

George slaps his face.

Peter holds his cheek, startled, then jumps and runs from the room. Wendy, bewildered, at the door, follows,

George holds out a key to no one in particular.

GEORGE

(*barely audible*)
Lock the door.

Lydia does so. George holds out other keys.

GEORGE

Now ... turn off the stoves, the
voice clocks, the talking books,
the TVs, the telephones, the
body scrubbers, the bedmakers,
turn off everything!

Lydia takes the keys, looks at George's face, and hurries away. Maclean looks after her.

> MACLEAN
>
> No, George. That was badly
> handled. Brutal . . . brutal!

Maclean hurries off after Lydia.

George, alone, rests his head against the playroom door, listening, eyes closed.

> GEORGE
>
> (*to himself*)
> Brutal? Yes, but dead! Are you
> dead in there?! Good.
> (*tiredly*)
> Good . . .

He moves away across the room, exhausted, and at the door turns to look back at the door.

> GEORGE
>
> I wonder . . . does the room hate
> me, too? Yes . . . it must. Nothing
> ever likes to die. Even a machine.

He exits.

Blackout.

Music in darkness.

A small bedlight comes slowly up after half a minute. We see Lydia in bed at the front of the stage. A dark scrim has come down between the bed and the set in back, so we do this scene in-one. Lydia rouses.

> LYDIA
>
> George?

She sees him to stage left now, back turned, in his dressing robe, looking out an imaginary window, smoking.

LYDIA

Can't sleep?

GEORGE

Who can?

LYDIA

Not me, anyway.

GEORGE

It's after midnight.

LYDIA

Yes. Listen. The house is so still.
  (*she sits up, listening*)
It used to hum all the time,
under its breath . . . I never
quite guessed the tune . . .
though I listened for years
and tried to hum the same way,
I never learned. . . .

GEORGE

Thank God for small favors.
Good Lord, it was strange, walking
around, shutting off all the
heaters and scrubbers and polishers,
and washers. For an hour there,
the house felt like a cemetery,
and me its keeper. That's past now.
I'm adjusting.

LYDIA

The children will, too. They cried themselves to
sleep, but they will forgive us.

She sits up listening as if she had heard something.

> LYDIA
>
> There's no way for them to—
> tamper—with the room, is there?

> GEORGE
>
> Tamper?

> LYDIA
>
> I just don't want them doing anything
> down there, messing about,
> rearranging things—they couldn't
> do anything to the room, could they?

> GEORGE
>
> *To* the room?
> What would they want to do *to* the
> room? Anyway, there's a lot of
> electricity in those walls with
> all the machinery. They know
> better than to mess, and get a
> nasty shock.

She listens again, and breaks up her own mood by trying to be jocular.

> LYDIA
>
> Oh, I'm glad we're leaving tomorrow,
> mountains, fishing, everything out
> in the open again after years.

> GEORGE
>
> Dave said he'd bring his
> helicopter round after breakfast
> and take us to the lake himself.
> Good old Dave!

George comes back to sit on the edge of his wife's bed.

GEORGE

Lydia?

LYDIA

Yes?

He takes her hand. He kisses her on the cheek. She jerks
away suddenly.

GEORGE

What is it?

LYDIA

Oh, listen, listen!

Far away, the sound of running antelope, the roar of lions.

WENDY and PETER
(*very remote*)
Help! Mother! Father!
Help! Help!

LYDIA

The children!

GEORGE

The playroom! They must have
broken into it!

PETER and WENDY
(*remote*)
Mother! Father, help, oh, help!

LYDIA

Peter! Wendy!

GEORGE

Kids! Kids! We're coming!
We're coming!

The parents rush off into darkness, as the lights go off
over the bed.

In the dark the voices continue.

PETER

Father, father, quick!
Quick!

GEORGE

Peter, Wendy!

LYDIA

Children, where are you?

WENDY

Here, oh, here!

The lights flash on; George and Lydia rush in through the playroom door.

GEORGE

They're in the playroom!

LYDIA

Peter! Wendy!

Once inside the door they peer around.

LYDIA

That's strange ...

GEORGE

I'd have sworn—

They look about to left and right and straight ahead through the fourth wall, at the audience.

LYDIA

George, it's—Africa again,
the sun, the veldt, the vultures ...

She backs off. George half turns and as he does so, the door slams shut behind them. George leaps toward it.

GEORGE

Damn door. A draft must have—

Locks click outside.

George tries the lock, beats at the door.

GEORGE

It's locked!

LYDIA

It can't be! There's no way
for it to lock itself!

GEORGE

(*thinking*)
No. . . . no . . .
Peter? Wendy?

LYDIA

George, over there, under the
trees . . .

GEORGE

Kids, open up . . .
I know you're out there.

LYDIA

The lions . . . they're walking out
into the sun . . .

GEORGE

(*shaking the door*)
Peter, Wendy, now don't be ridiculous.
Unlock this door!

The light is getting brighter in the room, the sun is blaz-
ing from above. The sound of the rustling vulture wings
grows louder. Shadows flash across the faces of George
and Lydia. The rumbling of the lions is nearer.

LYDIA

George, the lions, they're running
toward us!

George looks out through the fourth wall, grows uneasy,
somewhat panicky, and bangs at the door.

GEORGE

It's all right, Lydia.
Children, damn you, you're
frightening your mother, open up!
You hear?

LYDIA

Running! Running! Near! Near!

GEORGE

Peter!

LYDIA

Oh, George, the screams, the
screams. I know now what I never
said . . . the screams were familiar
. . . the voices . . . because the voices,
the screams were us, you and me,
George, you and me . . .

GEORGE

No! Kids! Hear me!

He bangs the door, turns, freezes, horrified.

LYDIA

George, stop them running, stop
them, stop, stop!

She throws up her hands to guard her face, sinks to her
knees.

LYDIA

They're going to jump!
Stop, stop!

GEORGE

No, they can't, they can't!
No! no!

The light blazes, the lions roar! A great shadow rushes
from the audience, as if the lions, in a solid pack, were
engulfing the stage in darkness!

Swallowing blackness takes all light away.

In the darkness, Lydia and George scream and scream.
Then abrupt silence, the roar, the bumbling purr of the
yellow beasts fading away.

After a long while of silence, a helicopter lands nearby.
We hear David Maclean calling in the darkness.

MACLEAN

(*easily*)
George! Lydia! I'm here!
George? Lydia?

The lights come slowly up. We are still inside the playroom. Seated facing the audience on two corduroy pillows
are Peter and Wendy, their faces impassive, as if they
had gone through all that life might ever do to them and
were beyond hearing, seeing, feeling. On a pillow between
them are small cups and saucers, a sugar and creamer set,
and a porcelain pot. Wendy holds one cup and saucer in
her frozen hands, as does Peter.

The door to the playroom opens. Maclean peers in, does
not see the children immediately.

MACLEAN

George—

He stops, peering off into the distance, as across a veldt.
We hear the faint roar of lions. He hears the flap of vulture wings sailing down the sky, and looks up into the

burning sun, protecting his eyes. Then at last he looks over at the children, sees them, and in his face is the beginning of realization, of horror, of insight into what they have done.

MACLEAN

(*slowly*)
Peter? ... Wendy ... ?

Peter turns his head slowly to look beyond the man.

PETER

Mr. Maclean.

Wendy turns more slowly, in shock, to hold out before her the small cup, her eyes blind to any sight, her voice toneless.

WENDY

A cup of tea?

Blackout.

THE END

To the Chicago Abyss

The curtain rises.

The empty stage represents a park. There is a bench at far-stage left and another at far-stage right. On the left sits a middle-aged woman who is busy taking a knitted sweater apart, unweaving the yarn, and rolling it into an unclean ball. She carries knitting needles with her and it is obvious she intends to reknit the yarn into a new garment once she finishes the destruction of the original sweater.

On the right bench a young man leans over drawing in the dust with a stick, very intent, very much to himself.

The old man enters now, gazing all about as if he wanted to see everything, looking ahead, looking behind, looking up, looking down. On his way perhaps he finds an old gum or candy wrapper, peers at it with admiration and puts it in his pocket for later reference. He is dressed poorly, his clothes are stiff and ancient with dirt, his feet are not so much in shoes as they are repaired, tacked together, and bandaged in leather and black friction tape.

As the old man moves, he seems alert for something, as if he had been searching for years, and might have to search many more years. His mouth and eyes are almost apprehensive. His eyes dart. His mouth trembles, as he talks to himself, as if there was much he wished to say, but could not bring it out.

Now, in the middle of the stage, he looks around. Though he does not speak yet, we read the desolation of the city in his face. He turns in a slow circle, as if surveying the city and his eyes tell us that the place is dead. He cannot bear to look at it. He glances now, instead, with vitality renewed, at either bench. He must decide where to sit. He chooses the bench with the woman on it and very quietly, with a slight bow, which she does not acknowledge, approaches, and sits at the far end away from her. She goes on taking the sweater apart.

The old man waits, not looking at her. He shuts his eyes. His mouth works for a long while. His head moves as if his nose were printing a single word on the air, invisible, before him. When he is done printing the word, he mouths it, silently. Then, eyes still shut, sitting up straight, in a loud clear voice he makes his announcement:

THE OLD MAN

Coffee!

The woman gasps and stiffens, she ceases work, but does not look at him. Eyes still shut, he goes on.

THE OLD MAN

Twist the key! Hissss!
Bright red, yellow-letter can!
Compressed air. Ssssst! Like
a snake, a snake! Psssss!

The woman snaps her head about as if slapped, to stare in dreadful fascination at the old man's moving tongue, his hands tumbling in pantomime on his lap.

THE OLD MAN

The odor, the scent, the smell,
the aroma of rich dark wondrous
Brazilian beans, fresh ground!

The woman leaps up, reeling as if gun-shot, steadying herself on the back of the bench. Her yarn ball falls to the ground. The old man, feeling her leap, opens his eyes. Perhaps he hopes to make her sit back now, just by talking her down.

THE OLD MAN

(*sniffs*)
The first sniff.
Ah,
like the warm air rising off the
dusky earth in hot summer twilight. Coffee. Coffee . . .

That does it. She breaks to run, remembers her yarn, turns,
is afraid to reach for it.

THE OLD MAN
No, don't . . . please . . .

She scrabbles for it. He hands it to her. She grabs it
and bolts off.

THE OLD MAN
Please, I didn't mean. You needn't—
(*resigned*)
Gone.

Which indeed she is, clutching her goods, looking back at
him as if he were insane.

The old man watches her out of sight, half-risen from the
bench, his hand out to plead after her. Now, weighted
with her desertion, he sinks to the bench again and remains, giving one great silent exhalation. Then, from the
corner of his eyes, he sees the other bench. He sits up.
He straightens his shoulders. He rises and with great un-
concern, picking up pieces of paper and pocketing them
or throwing them away as he chooses, approaches the
other bench where the young man, not seeing him, has
stopped drawing in the dust and has taken out some dried
grass which he is rolling into a thin piece of old newsprint
or toilet paper, making himself a poor imitation of a
cigarette.

The old man watches, intrigued, standing just beyond the bench, until the young man finally finds a match on his person and lights the cigarette, leans back, squinting deliciously, blowing smoke. As the smoke dissolves in the air, the old man watches the patterns and says, as if this touched his memory unbeknownst:

THE OLD MAN
Chesterfields.

The young man, the cigarette clenched in his mouth, grips his knees with his hands.

THE OLD MAN
Raleighs. Lucky Strikes.

The old man, not really talking to anyone but himself, not putting on a performance for anyone, but just living in another day, another time, continues, sitting down now as if the young man weren't really there, even though the young man is staring at him.

THE OLD MAN
Kents. Kools, Marlboros. Those
were the names. Pall Malls. Old
Golds. White, red, amber packs,
grass green, sky blue, pure gold
with the red slick small ribbon
that ran around the top you pulled
to zip away the crinkly cellophane
like soft glass, and then the blue
government tax stamp, and the tin-
foil you saved in a big bright
silver ball and sold to the junkman
and—

THE YOUNG MAN
(*coldly*)
Shut up.

THE OLD MAN

(*hasn't heard*)
... buy them in drugstores,
fountains, subways ...

THE YOUNG MAN

Quiet!

The old man opens his eyes, surprised that someone has
called. He looks to see the young man's expression, his
open and irritable mouth. He sizes up the situation.

THE OLD MAN

Gently ...

THE YOUNG MAN

Gently, he says. Gently.
He doesn't even know where
he is and gently ...

THE OLD MAN

I'm in the park, in the city.

THE YOUNG MAN

What park? What city?
Look *up* for a change instead
of running around like a damn
hound dog, your nose on the
ground.

THE OLD MAN

I'm *looking* up.

THE YOUNG MAN

Whatta you see out there?

THE OLD MAN

Buildings ...

THE YOUNG MAN

No, ruins!

THE OLD MAN

Streets . . .

THE YOUNG MAN

No, bomb craters.

THE OLD MAN

I'm sorry. It was such a nice
friendly day—

THE YOUNG MAN

I'm no friend.

THE OLD MAN

We're all friends now, or why live?

THE YOUNG MAN

Some friend. Look what you made
me do. Ruined my smoke.
   (*he brushes the cigarette "makings" off his*
   pants, angrily)
Who knows friends?
Who *had* one?
Back in 1970, maybe, sure—

THE OLD MAN

1970. You must have been a baby then.
Why, they still had Butterfingers that
year in bright yellow wrappers. Baby
Ruths. Clark Bars in orange paper.
Milky Ways . . . swallow a universe of
stars, comets, meteors . . .
   (*he unwraps an imaginary bar, bites it, chews*)
Nice . . .

THE YOUNG MAN

It was never nice. What's wrong with
you?

THE OLD MAN

I remember limes and lemons, that's
what's wrong with me. Do you remember
oranges?

(*picks one off the air*)

THE YOUNG MAN

Damn right. Oranges. Hell. You calling me liar? You want me to feel bad?
You nuts? Don't you know the law? You
know I could turn you in, don't you?

THE OLD MAN

I know, I know. The weather fooled me.
It made me want to compare—

THE YOUNG MAN

Compare rumors, that's what the police'd
say, huh, eh? The special cops'd say
"rumors," you troublemaking bastard,
you—

He seizes the old man's lapels which rip so the young
man has to grab a second handful, yelling down into his
face.

THE YOUNG MAN

Why don't I just blast the
living Jesus out of you. I
ain't hurt no one in *so long* . . .

He shoves the old man, which gives him the idea to pum-
mel, which in turn gives him the idea to punch and then
rain blows upon the old man's shoulders, arms, chest.
The old man tries to fend off this rain of assault.

THE YOUNG MAN

Candies, damn it, smokes, damn
you! Kents! Kools! Baby Ruths,

Butterfingers! Kents Kools Butterfingers! Butterfingers!

The old man slips and falls to roll over, balling himself
up, for the young man is starting to kick but stops
now, for he is sobbing. The old man looks up, surprised,
and takes his hands away from his face.

> THE OLD MAN
> Please . . .

The young man weeps louder, turning away.

> THE OLD MAN
> It's my fault. I apologize. I
> didn't want to make anyone cry.
> Don't. We won't be hungry forever.

The old man is sitting up as he talks.

> THE OLD MAN
> We'll rebuild the cities. Listen.
> No crying. I just wanted people
> to think where are we going, what
> are we doing, what've we done? You
> weren't hitting me, anyway. You
> meant to hit something else, the
> Time, huh, the way things are? But
> who can hit Time, hit the way things
> are? I was handy. But look, I'm
> sitting up fine . . . I . . .

The young man has stopped crying during this and now
breaks in.

> THE YOUNG MAN
> You . . . you can't go around making people
> unhappy. I'll find someone to fix you.

I'll find . . . someone!
>(*exits*)
Someone!

THE OLD MAN

Wait! No, no!

But, still on his knees, he cannot pursue. The young man has run off, shouting. His shouting fades.

THE STRANGER
>(*nearby; quietly*)
Fool.

The old man, feeling his bones, looks around. The stranger, about 40, having entered during the brawl, has stood behind the farthest bench, in shadow, watching.

THE OLD MAN

Beg pardon?

STRANGER

I said: Fool.

THE OLD MAN
You were there, all the time,
you saw, and did *nothing?*

STRANGER
What, fight one fool to save
another? No.

He walks forward to help the old man to his feet, and brush him off.

STRANGER
No, I save my fighting for where
it pays. Come on. You're going
with me.

THE OLD MAN

Where? Why?

STRANGER

Where? Home. Why? That scum'll
be back with the police any minute.
I don't want you stolen away, you're
a very precious commodity. I've
heard of you for months, searched
for you for days. Then just when I
find you, good grief, you're up to
your famous tricks. What did you
say made that boy mad?

THE OLD MAN

I said about oranges and lemons,
candy, cigarettes. I was just
getting ready to recollect wind-
up toys, briar pipes and back
scratchers, when he dropped the
sky on me.

STRANGER
(*handing over a handkerchief*)
I almost don't blame him. I almost
wanted to hit you, myself. There's
a siren! Double-time. Out of the
park!

The old man, the bloodied handkerchief to his ruined
mouth, allows himself to be led, but stops and bends.

THE OLD MAN

Wait! I can't leave this behind.
Very precious stone, very precious!

They both stare at it.

THE OLD MAN

(*proudly*)
My tooth!

He tosses it in the air, grabs it in a tight fist, and together they hurry from the park, as the siren rises.

Blackout . . . or swirling shadows as a door, or several doors come down out of darkness, a table and some chairs slide in, and suddenly a seedy and ill-kempt apartment has swarmed to steady itself and fall into focus about the old man. He stands looking at the table and chair as if not knowing what to do with them. The stranger gives him a hint.

STRANGER

Sit down.

THE OLD MAN

Yes. Thank you.

STRANGER

There's food.

THE OLD MAN

Food? I don't know. My mouth—

STRANGER

Wine, then, until your mouth
feels better. Dear?

His wife, standing near, remembers the wine bottle and the single glass in her hand, pours, hands it to the old man.

THE OLD MAN

Wine? I can't believe it.
Aren't you having any?

STRANGER
(*laughing*)
We have only one glass. We'll
have to share our toast. No,
you first.

The old man sips, eyes shut.

THE OLD MAN
Wine. Wine. Incredible.
To you, kind lady, kind sir.

He sips, and passes the glass to the woman, who drinks
timidly and passes it to her husband who also drinks.

STRANGER
To all of us. To other years.
To old men who talk too much.
To pummelings, beatings, and
lost teeth.

The wife drops a plate on the table, at this.

STRANGER
Relax. No one followed us.
Set the table, put out the food.

She brings dishes and food to the table. The old man
watches her, fascinated.

STRANGER
Old man, the beating, how did it
happen? Why do you behave like a
saint panting after martyrdom?
You're famous, you know. Everyone's
heard of you. Many would like to
meet you. Myself, first, I want to
know what makes you tick. Well?

But the old man is counting as the woman puts the food out on the plate with a fork.

THE OLD MAN

17, 18, 19 strands of spaghetti.
25, 26, 27, 28, 29 green peas.
(*glances up*)
Forgive me. But I shall pray over these like
a fine rosary! 19 strings
of spaghetti, 29 peas,
and—no—one meat ball! What a
still life. How fine!

The others pull up their chairs.

THE OLD MAN

But, madame, you have only 28
peas, and you, sir, 27!
It's not fair I have 29.

THE WIFE

You are the guest.

THE OLD MAN

So I am, and most grateful.

He touches the peas with a fork, gingerly, reminiscently.

THE OLD MAN

29 peas. Remember, remember.
A motion picture I saw as a child.
A comedian in the film—do you know
the word "comedian"? A funny man to
make you laugh—this comedian met a
lunatic in a midnight haunted house
in this film and—

The stranger and his wife have laughed, tentatively, quietly.

THE OLD MAN

(*abashed*)

I'm sorry, that's not the joke yet.

(*clears his throat, squints to remember*)

The lunatic sat the
comedian down to an empty table, no
knives, no forks, no food! "Dinner
is served!" he cried. Afraid of
murder, the comedian fell in with the
make-believe. "Great!" he cried,
pretending to chew steak, vegetables,
dessert. He bit into nothings.
"Fine!" He swallowed air. "Wonderful!"

(*pause*)

You may laugh now.
Eh . . .

But the husband and wife, grown still, only look at their
sparsely strewn plates. The old man, disquieted at what
he has done with the tale, tries to carry it on, cheer them
up.

THE OLD MAN

The comedian, thinking to impress
the madman, exclaimed, "And these
spiced peaches! Superb!" "Peaches?"
screamed the madman, and drew a
pistol. "I served no peaches. You
must be nuts!" And shot the comedian
in the behind.

The old man laughs in a kind of half-gasped quiet laugh-
ter, at the same time picking up and weighing one pea on
his fork. He is about to put it in his mouth when—

Bam! a terrible ramming knock once, pause, once twice,
on the slatty door!

POLICEMAN

(*outside*)
Special police!

In one flowing motion the lights shift, and move toward
dusk, the old man rises, automatically taking his plate and
fork with him, the wife moves toward the spotlighted door
on stage right, the husband steers the old man toward a
wall at midstage and as the wife touches the front door,
a panel opens in the wall and the old man steps through
as the wife opens the front door and the panel slides shut
hiding the old man. The panel is scrim, and, illumined
from behind, we can see the old man standing abandoned,
the plate in one hand, the fork in the other.

As the special policeman steps through the door, the lighting changes even more, getting darker, except where he
stands. The husband and wife, moving off, stand far over
on stage left, as if not wishing to be anywhere near the
policeman. They move into dark, as it were, so he cannot
search their faces too carefully as they talk. The policeman probes about with a flashlight.

POLICEMAN

Special police.

STRANGER

You said that.

POLICEMAN

I'll say it again, and you'll
listen. Special police. And
I'm looking for a criminal fugitive.

THE OLD MAN

(*to himself, listening*)
Isn't this world full of criminal
fugitives?

As the policeman talks and the stranger and his wife listen, the old man, hidden between, behind the scrim panel wall, turns now this way, now that, cupping an ear on occasion, listening, responding. We can hear his response, but know that the policeman and the couple cannot.

> POLICEMAN
> A man in patched and dirty clothes—

> THE OLD MAN
> (*to himself*)
> I thought *everyone's* clothes were
> patched and dirty!

> POLICEMAN
> —an old old man—

> THE OLD MAN
> But isn't *everyone* old?

> POLICEMAN
> If you turn him in, there's
> a week's rations as reward.

The old man quickens at this, as do the stranger and his wife.

> THE WIFE
> A week's rations!!?

> STRANGER
> (*cutting across her*)
> He—he must be Much Wanted.

> POLICEMAN
> (*consulting his dossier*)
> Much.

> THE WIFE
> (*musing*)
> A week's rations.

THE OLD MAN
(*amazed himself*)
A whole week!

POLICEMAN
(*sensing his line is good*)
Plus!!

THE OLD MAN
Plus?

POLICEMAN
A bonus of ten cans of vegetable
soup and five cans of beans!

STRANGER
(*in spite of himself*)
Soup?

THE WIFE
Beans?

THE OLD MAN
Real tin cans, it must be, real cans
with bright red labels. Cans that
flash like silver meteors, oh I can
see them even in the dark. What a
fine reward. Not $10,000
for the old talking man, no, no, not
$20,000, but . . . some-
thing that *counts,* that really *means*
something . . . ten incredible cans of
real not imitation soup, and five,
count them, five brilliant circus-
colored cans of exotic beans. *Think*
of it. *Think!*

There is a long silence in which the husband and wife
lean all unawares toward the policeman.

POLICEMAN
Think of it! Think!

THE OLD MAN
I *am*. They *are*. Listen. The
faint murmurs of stomachs turning
all uneasy. Too many years the
world has fed them hairballs of
nightmare and politics gone sour,
a thin gruel. Now, their lips work,
their saliva runs like Niagara!

The policeman listens as if he can hear their appetites at
work, then turns and with his back to them, hand on the
door, says,

POLICEMAN
Beans. Soup. Fifteen solid-pack cans!

Slam, he is out the door, gone. *Bang*, he knocks on other
far doors, *bang, bang*.

POLICEMAN
(*fading away*)
Special police . . . special police . . .

They listen to the fading sound until it is absolutely gone.
Then they relax their knotted fists, and unlean their bodies.
The secret panel whispers up. The husband and wife cannot bring themselves to look at the old man who stands
there looking at them and then at the pitiful plate of food
and the fork in his two hands. He does not move for a
long time.

THE OLD MAN
(*gently, in awe*)
Even I . . . even *I* was tempted to turn
myself in, claim the reward, eat the
soup . . .

He moves out to touch at their elbows, each in turn.

THE OLD MAN
Why? Why didn't you hand me over?

The husband breaks away, impulsively, as if he must. He rushes to the table in a terrible hunger and crams all the food in his mouth as if to stave off his awful fear, need, and appetite.

STRANGER
Eat! Eat! You'll find out. Wife, go
on, you know what to do, get!

The wife hesitates and goes out.

THE OLD MAN
(*worried*)
Where is she—?

STRANGER
Eat, old man, eat!

The old man brings his plate forward and, nonplused, picks at the food.

THE OLD MAN
Your wife—?

STRANGER
She's gone to get the Others.

THE OLD MAN
(*half-rising*)
Others!?

STRANGER
Everyone in the apartment house.

THE OLD MAN
(*really on his feet now*)
Everyone!!??

STRANGER

Old man, look, if you're going to
run risks, shoot off your mouth,
why not do it in the aggregate, one
fell blow? Why waste your breath
on one or two people if—

There are noises of people now approaching, murmuring,
a shuffling of feet, and many shadows. The old man looks
around as if the room were filling.

THE OLD MAN

Yes, but what shall I *tell* them?

STRANGER

What *won't* you tell them! Isn't
this better than taking a chance
in the open?

The crowd is coming in, unseen, with murmurs, shadows.
The old man is still bewildered, uncertain.

THE OLD MAN

(*half-nods*)
Yes. Strange. I hate pain. I hate
being hit and chased. But my tongue
moves ...

STRANGER

(*encouraging him*)
Yes, that's it ...

THE OLD MAN

... I must hear what it has to say ...

STRANGER

(*egging him on*)
That's it!

The old man looks around as the shadows move and the crowd begins to quiet. He pecks at his food, uncertainly.

> STRANGER
> (*still trying to distract him*)
> That's no way to eat! *Shovel* it in!

As if needing this sustenance and to break the spell, the old man loads his fork.

> THE OLD MAN
> One shovel and it's gone.
> (*shrugs*)
> So . . . one shovel.
> (*eats*)

And as he swallows, the weight of the food, it almost seems, sinks him down into the chair and gives him strength at the same time, and the crowd is there now, all about we see their shadows, and the wife enters and nods.

At her nod, the crowd goes to complete waiting silence. Surrounded by their breathing, the old man is uneasy somewhat, still.

The stranger, sensing this, half-attacks.

> THE STRANGER
> Now tell me, why are you such a damn
> fool you make *us* damn fools seek you
> out and risk our necks to bring you
> here, eh? Well . . . ?

The old man, looking around, recalls something, his eyes half-light, he shakes his head with recollection.

> THE OLD MAN
> Why . . . it's almost like the theater . . .
> motion-picture houses . . .

THE STRANGER
(*urging this on*)
Drive-in movies, too, yes, yes . . .

The old man gazes about, half-pleased, half-afraid, both
in and out of other years now. He rises, steps forward.

THE OLD MAN
But . . . the show . . . the entertainment . . . why . . .
it's . . . *me!*

The crowd murmurs a bit in response, eager, and the old
man puts down his empty plate as if gathering his
resources. He nods sadly, going back in his mind. He half-
squints his eyes.

THE OLD MAN
Yes, yes. The hour grows late in the
day, the sun is down the sky, and soon,
in the evening hours, with the lights dim,
the entertainment begins, the show starts,
the wonders commence, things will be said,
people will hold hands and listen like the
old days with the balconies and the dark,
or the cars and the dark . . . And in the
midst of the smell of popcorn and spearmint
gum and orange crush . . . the show begins . . .

Now, thoroughly oriented, the old man looks up out of
his own depths and is ready for the performance. Slowly
he looks at his audience, to the left, to the right and
straight ahead. He glances at the stranger, then forgets
him and talks.

THE OLD MAN
Fool. That's what you called me. I
accept the name. Well then, how did
I *start* my foolishness? Years ago, I

looked at the ruined world, the
dictatorships, the dead states, the empty
nations, and said, "What can I do? Me, a
tired old man, what? Rebuild a devastation?
Ha!" But lying half asleep one night I
remembered a phonograph record I once owned . . .

He lifts the wife's hand like a phonograph-arm and her
fingertip the needle. He cranks the air. He puts her "needle"
finger down.

THE OLD MAN

The phonograph, the record. What a phonograph, what a song! An ancient vaudeville
team, the Duncan Sisters!

The record hisses and we hear the Duncan sisters, singing.

THE SONG

"Remembering, is all I do, dear
Remembering" . . . etc.

THE OLD MAN

You hear that? Hear some *more!*

They listen, the old man sways, almost dances.

THE OLD MAN

Remembering? Remembering. I sang the
song. Remembering. And suddenly it
wasn't a song, it was a *way of life!*

STRANGER

A way of life?

THE OLD MAN

What did I have to offer a world
that was forgetting? My memory!
How could my memory help? By

offering comparisons! By tell-
ing the young what *once* was. By
considering our losses! I found
the more I remembered, the more I
could remember! Millions of things.

STRANGER
Like what?

The music has faded, but remains as a ghost echo all
through the following:

THE OLD MAN
Like . . . imitation flowers.

Suddenly he has some in his hand.

THE OLD MAN
Kazoos. You ever *play* a kazoo?

He produces one and plays "Remembering" for a few notes.

THE OLD MAN
Jew's harps . . . !
Harmonicas!

He produces both.

THE OLD MAN
Thimbles! How long since you saw,
if you *ever did see,* a thimble!

Like a sorcerer he produces one, two, three, four, five
thimbles, one for each finger and thumb of his left hand.

THE OLD MAN
Bicycle clips, not bicycles, no,
but *first* bicycle *clips!*

These he clips onto his pants.

THE OLD MAN

Antimacassars. Do you *know*
them??? Giant snowflakes for
the furniture! And . . . !
Once a man asked me to remember
just the dashboard dials on a
Cadillac. I remembered. I told
him in detail. He listened. He
cried great tears down his face.
Happy tears or sad? I can't say.
I only remember.
Not literature, no. I never had
a head for plays or poems, they
slip away, they die. All I am,
really, is a trash-heap of the
mediocre, the third-rate-hand-me-
down, useless and chromed-over
slush and junk of a racetrack
civilization that ran "last" over
a precipice and still hasn't struck
bottom. So all I can offer really
is scintillant junk, the clamored-
after chronometers and absurd
machineries of a never-ending river
of robots and robot-mad owners.
Yet, one way or another, civilization
must get back on the road. Those who
can offer fine butterfly poetry, let
them remember, let them offer. Those
who can weave and build butterfly nets,
let them weave, let them build. My
gift is smaller than both, and perhaps
contemptible in the long hoist, climb,
jump, toward the old and amiably silly

peak. But I *must* dream myself worthy.
For the things, silly or not, that
people remember are the things they
will search for again.
I will then ulcerate the people's
half-dead desires with vinegar-gnat
memory. So perhaps they'll rattle-
bang the Big Clock together again,
which is the City, the State, and
then the World. Let one man want
wine, another lounge chairs, a third
a batwing glider to soar the March
winds on and so you build even
greater electropterodactyls to
scour even greater winds with even
greater peoples—
Someone wants moron Christmas trees
and some wise man goes to cut them.
Pack this all together, wheel in
wheel, want in want, and I'm there
to oil and keep it running. Ho, once
I would have raved, "Only the *best* is
best, only *quality* is true!" But
roses grow from blood manure. Mediocre
must be, so most-excellent fine can
bloom. And I shall be the Best Mediocre
there is and fight all who say, "Slide
under, sink back, dust-wallow, let
brambles scurry over your living grave!"
I shall protest the roving apeman tribes,
the sheep-people munching the far fields
preyed on by the feudal land-baron wolves
who rarefy themselves in the few sky-

scraper summits and hoard unremembered
foods. And these villains I will kill
with can opener and corkscrew, I shall
run down with ghosts of Buick, Kissel-
Car, and Moon, thrash them with licorice
whips until they cry "Mercy!" Can one
do this?

He surveys the full panoply of memories hung upon his
inner eye. He finishes:

THE OLD MAN

. . . one can only try.

The old man stands among his memories in a moment of
silence.

Someone clears his throat.

The old man starts out of his spell. The crowd murmurs.

The old man and the stranger look around as if not guess-
ing the reaction of the audience, which murmurs louder
now, half like a disturbed or perhaps wounded but perhaps placated and petted Beast, not knowing whether to
applaud the poetry or damn the sad upheaval of old
memory!

THE STRANGER

Old man . . .

THE OLD MAN
(*looking around*)

What did I *say?*

THE STRANGER

You'd better go now—

THE OLD MAN

Did they *hear* me?

THE STRANGER

They—

THE OLD MAN

Did they *understand?* What—?

The stranger takes his elbow and thrusts a folded red ticket, very long and bright, upon him.

THE STRANGER

To be on the safe side—

THE OLD MAN

Safe side . . . ?

THE STRANGER

Here's a ticket from a friend of mine in Transportation. One train crosses the country each week. Each week I get a free pass for some idiot I want to help. *This* week, it's *you*.

THE OLD MAN

(*taking the paper*)
Me? Ticket? . . .
(*reads*)
"One-way to Chicago Abyss."
(*glances up*)
Is the Abyss still *there?*

THE STRANGER

(*trying to move him,*

glancing around uneasily at the audience
now himself, which still murmurs)
Yes, yes. This time next year, Lake
Michigan may break through the last
crust and make a new lake in the bomb
crater where the city once was. There's
life of sorts around the crater rim, and
a branch train runs west once a month.
After you leave here, keep moving . . .

THE OLD MAN

Moving . . . ?

THE STRANGER

Forget you met or know us.

THE OLD MAN

Forget?!
(*almost laughs at the suggestion*)
Me?!

THE STRANGER

And for God's sake, for the next year in
the open, alone, declare a moratorium.
Keep your fine mouth shut.
(*hands over a second, yellow card*)
And here. This is a dentist I know near
Kansas Trace. Tell him to make you a
new set of teeth that will only open at
mealtimes.

The old man has been pushed and urged toward the door,
but cannot resist looking back, out and around.

THE OLD MAN
Oh, God. *Did* they hear? *Do* they *know?*

The crowd becomes dreadfully still, cuts off. Silence. A
beat. The old man stares as if to fathom them. He looks
at the red ticket. Then, seizing the stranger's hand and
arm, he shakes, he wrings it in terrible friendship, and . . .

Bolts! Runs off as if wildly pursued.

Swift running darkness!

A locomotive whistle, the sound of a train rushing on
tracks.

Somehow, we find a train, or the echo of a train, the
phantom semblance of a train, is under and around the
old man. He sways. The night sweeps by, running in a
blizzard of snowflakes and sound.

Standing, swaying amidst all this, among crumpled masses
of clothing which must be people crammed into a narrow
room, and on benches, the old man speaks to the night
and the running train, peering first, in awe, at the ticket
in his hand, reading the words to believe them, then looking around at his swift, strange environment . . .

THE OLD MAN
(*to himself*)
. . . Chicago Abyss . . .
night . . . time . . . snow . . . a blizzard
of cold snow falling on the earth . . .
ancient train . . . old cars . . . crammed
with unwashed people . . . hundreds,
thousands . . . sleeping in the aisles,
jammed in the rest rooms, fighting
to sleep, hoping not to dream . . .

He looks around, as if suddenly reminded of something, as he finds a place for himself jammed among the ragbags which must be sleeping humans.

THE OLD MAN
(*to himself as he sits*)
Remember, quiet, shut up, no, don't
speak, nothing, stay still, think,
careful . . . cease . . .

The train roars its whistle, flashes over a viaduct with new disturbs of thunder, fades, the old man sways.

THE OLD MAN
(*to himself*)
Wait . . . wait . . .

For now a light has come slowly on to show us a boy of some 10 or 11 years, who is sitting near the old man, watching him with a steady gaze. He has been watching during all the above, but only now does his gaze, like a beacon, pick out the old man and cause him to cease communing with himself. Now the light is very bright upon the boy; he becomes the most important thing on the train. The rest of the lights, showing us the crowded humanity on the floors and benches, begin to fade now. The sound of the train is a muted humming dream.

Fascinated, the old man looks at the boy who looks back, unblinking, his eyes wide, his face pale, his ticket clenched in his hand, a look of great lost loneliness and traveling by himself in his gaze.

The old man turns away, shuts his eyes. The boy looks at him. The old man turns back, looks at the boy, and again turns away.

The boy watches him.

The old man opens his eyes, argues with himself, moving his lips . . . but we cannot hear what he says . . . we only see him shrug, almost hit at his own arms, and firmly resolve not to look at the boy. Again he glances over at the boy but more swiftly now turns away, for the boy has not blinked and still fixes him with a clear pale look.

At last, looking around, to see if all are asleep, and no one is listening, the old man looks at the boy again, swallows, wets his lips, revs up his courage, and speaks.

>   THE OLD MAN
>   (*leaning forward*)
>   Shh, boy. Your *name?*

The train roars up a bit, fades. The boy waits and speaks.

>   THE BOY
>   Joseph.

The train sways and creaks, snow light falls down in a silent blizzard of Time around them.

>   THE OLD MAN
>   Joseph . . . ?
>   (*he nods*)
>   Ah . . .

He looks around one last time and leans further forward toward that pale face, those great round bright waiting eyes.

>   THE OLD MAN
>   Well, Joseph . . .

The old man lifts his fingers softly on the air.

THE OLD MAN
... once upon a time ...

All freezes in tableau. The lights dim.

In the dark, the train runs away and away, fading, with a last cry of its lost whistle.

By which time the curtain has come down and we are at

THE END

ABOUT THE AUTHOR

RAY DOUGLAS BRADBURY was born in Waukegan, Illinois, in 1920. He graduated from a Los Angeles high school in 1938. His formal education ended there, but he furthered it by himself at night in the library, and during the day at his typewriter.

He sold newspapers on Los Angeles street corners from 1938 to 1942. His first science-fiction story was published in 1941. He has won many awards, among them the O'Henry Memorial Award, The Benjamin Franklin Award in 1954, and The Aviation-Space Writer's Association Award for the best space article in an American magazine in 1967. He has been published in every major American magazine over the years.

Among his most celebrated books published by Bantam are *The Martian Chronicles, Dandelion Wine, The Illustrated Man, The Golden Apples of the Sun* and *A Medicine for Melancholy.*